NORFOLK VILLAGES

OTHER BOOKS IN THE VILLAGE SERIES

Cornish Villages
Donald R. Rawe
Cotswold Villages
June R. Lewis
Cumbrian Villages
Kenneth Smith
Devon Villages
S. H. Burton
Dorset Villages
Roland Gant
Durham Villages
Harry Thompson
Highland Villages
James Shaw Grant
Kent Villages
Alan Bignell
Lancashire Villages
Jessica Lofthouse
Lowland Scottish Villages
Maurice Lindsay
Northumberland Villages
Godfrey Watson
Shropshire and Herefordshire Villages
George H. Haines
Suffolk Villages
Allan Jobson
Surrey Villages
Derek Pitt and Michael Shaw
Sussex Villages
Michael H. C. Baker
Yorkshire Villages
G. Bernard Wood

Other books by David H. Kennett
Anglo-Saxon Pottery
Portrait of Bedfordshire
Barracuda Guide to County History. Volume V: Bedfordshire
Victorian and Edwardian Horses from Old Photographs

Norfolk Villages

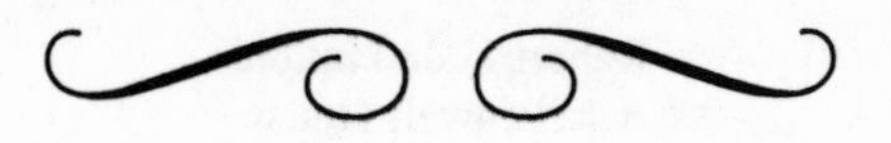

DAVID H. KENNETT

ROBERT HALE : LONDON

First published in Great Britain 1980

ISBN 0 7091 8129 9

Robert Hale Limited
Clerkenwell House
Clerkenwell Green
London EC1R 0HT

PRINTED IN GREAT BRITAIN BY
CLARKE, DOBLE & BRENDON LTD.
PLYMOUTH AND LONDON

Contents

Illustrations

Between pages 68 and 69

Between pages 100 and 101

LIST OF ILLUSTRATIONS

MAP

PICTURE CREDITS

All photographs were taken by the author

For Maria Howes
Born in a Norfolk Village
28 July 1884
An affectionate and much-loved
Great Aunt
The last of her generation of
a Norfolk family

Acknowledgements

Norfolk is a large county; to know it fully is difficult and to explore its ways for this book I chose perhaps not the simplest of transport. The Eastern Counties Omnibus Company still runs to many Norfolk villages. It seems appropriate to begin my thanks with them and particularly with the drivers of one-man-operated buses who have set me down and picked me up at places as diverse as Hellington Corner and Holkham, to name but two, and batted not an eyelid when a stranger with two bags—one with the camera, the other with the sandwiches and tea flasks—wished to alight there. I owe an especial debt to the drivers of route 619 who regularly sold me a 'Wanderbus' ticket, three or four days a week for ten weeks. Where the bus does not go, I walked. Only once did I become stranded; to the kind lady in Reepham library who gave me a lift to Aylsham, on a cold August day, I am most grateful. My father kindly drove me to a number of distant and remote villages, along roads which are not always conducive to good driving. My parents allowed me to occupy their spare bed for most of the summer of 1978.

For assistance over books and factual information I am obliged to the Great Yarmouth Public Library and the Rye and Colman Libraries of Norwich City Library. The photographic collections of the latter were also searched. Luton Public Library arranged the loan of a large number of volumes and Luton Museum permitted me to raid their excellent collection of Victorian and later trade directories. Robert Irons turned my not always brilliant negatives into good prints for the illustrations.

My final thanks are most important. A young lady was

long-suffering. Susan Holland endured absences, grumpiness and introspection when present and all the other sins and evils of the writing life; yet she was still willing to come with me to cold Cley-next-the-Sea, wait in a noxious Norwich bus station while I went off to fragmented Forncett, and prepare the card indices from which some sections of this book were written. All that in addition to the traditional chore of the index and cooking food of undoubted distinction which I avidly consumed. The domestic strain on me was a great deal less and for that I am more than grateful.

I

Saxon and Dane: the Village Founders

VILLAGES and their sites belong not to time immemorial; the place of each human settlement has a definite beginning. In Norfolk, as elsewhere in England, the date of the foundation of the villages we have today lies somewhere between A.D. 600 and A.D. 800. Norfolk villages have no earlier beginning.

There is more than one earlier pattern of Norfolk villages, but they are not discussed in this book. David Yaxley in *Portrait of Norfolk* (Hale, 1977) gave a modern introduction to the archaeology of the county in Roman times and before, and what he has fully discussed I have tended to treat only lightly. One brief mention may be made of the pre-Roman Iron Age village at West Harling where a circular structure was discovered which may have been home to more than one family. It belongs a millennium before the arrival of the first Anglo-Saxon settlers in England; it and similar places have left only the slightest surface traces and, excepting the walls of Roman towns at Caistor St Edmund and Caistor-next-to-Yarmouth and the Roman fort at Burgh Castle, the earliest visible remains in Norfolk are those of the ninth century and beyond, the late Saxon period. To the late Saxon period also belongs the creation of towns as we know them: Thetford was among the places founded then as a town. Before then, all men lived in villages. The geography of their settlements, particularly those made in the fifth and sixth centuries by the first Anglo-Saxon settlers, is best discerned from the sites of their burial grounds. On the surface the pattern presented by Anglo-Saxon graveyards seems not unlike the modern map, but this is to take a superficial view. To study the earliest Saxon settlement of Norfolk it is necessary not only to look at the broad sweep of things but also to examine the relationship between early settlements and burial grounds on the one hand and much later parish boundaries on the other. These show a very different picture emerging. The broad sweep of generalization gives way to the narrow focus of the particular.

Examples can be taken from each of the constituent parts of the county, excepting the Fleggs—the traditional name for the hinterland of Great Yarmouth. Throughout this book the regions within Norfolk which are used are those designated by the local government reorganization of 1974. This gave Norfolk seven districts. Norwich is purely urban, and Great Yarmouth includes only a few villages close to the former county borough. The other five—West Norfolk, North Norfolk, Breckland, Broadland and South Norfolk—are largely composed of the eight hundred or so villages of the county. The first has three towns: King's Lynn, Hunstanton and Downham Market. Wells, Sheringham, Cromer and North Walsham are in North Norfolk, while Breckland includes Thetford, Swaffham and East Dereham. Broadland is without a major urban centre, relying heavily on Norwich, as in fact does South Norfolk, although Wymondham and Diss are within this district. These five districts contain the Norfolk villages.

Modern villages are on sites different from those the earliest English settlers founded. Castle Acre in West Norfolk is perhaps the best example. An Anglo-Saxon cemetery was found here in 1857 and investigated again in 1891 and 1961: the pottery surviving from the many cremations unearthed is at present being studied for total publication. The individual urns are of only passing interest to the general reader. Of much greater significance is the site of the cemetery. First discoveries were made when a new bank dividing two parishes was being made. Castle Acre adjoins West Acre; urns have been found in fields in both parishes, obviously from the same cemetery. Priory Field, the location of the discoveries in Castle Acre, is no less than two-and-a-half kilometres from the centre of the village; it is a similar distance from the centre of West Acre village. This is not the only site of an Anglo-Saxon cemetery found on a parish boundary in Norfolk. One cemetery has such a confused description that it is most frequently known as Fakenham or Pensthorpe, although perhaps it should most precisely be known as Kettlestone; it was found about 300 metres north-east of Pensthorpe Hall (which is in Kettlestone parish) and immediately east of The Heath, Fakenham. Like Castle Acre this is a cremation cemetry, although the West Norfolk site does not seem to have been marked by barrows as was the case at Kettlestone. A third example, again a cremation cemetery, can be given, this time from Broadland. Some time between 1880 and 1900 at least seven burial urns were discovered at Brundall Gardens which, as the still surviving railway halt makes clear, is on the western edge of Brundall parish.

Parishes and their boundaries became fixed during the Saxon age, but not in its earliest centuries. Norfolk, like the rest of England, saw a very large shift in the location of villages two hundred years or so after the migration of the English to Britain.

The probable sites of the villages of the earliest Saxon settlers in Norfolk are most easily recognized from their burial grounds. Three, all with the rite of cremation in urns, have been cited. However, not all the burials of Norfolk dating to the fifth and sixth centuries are cremations. One of the largest cemeteries yet found in the county is that excavated at Morningthorpe, South Norfolk, in 1974 and 1975. Here a sixth-century cemetery of 315 inhumation graves was excavated by Andrew Rogerson. The bodies had been buried, often in their clothes, but were not burnt. Much earlier in their date of discovery are two other sites: Brooke, again in South Norfolk, and Kenninghall, which is in the south-east corner of Breckland. A recent comment on the Brooke site suggested it was a small cemetery—the objects present seem to represent no more than twenty graves—of late sixth-century date; the Kenninghall cemetery was in use at the same time. Inhumation cemeteries have been found in other areas of Norfolk. Another sixth-century cemetery is that found at Sporle, West Norfolk, in 1820. These finds, like those from Brooke, can only be studied as a group of objects. The Morningthorpe cemetery reveals the value of modern excavations in understanding the Saxon settlement of an area.

So far I have consistently called the earliest English settlers of Norfolk "Saxon" or "Anglo-Saxon" but as every schoolboy knows Norfolk is one of the two counties of *East Anglia*, named after another of the peoples who came to Britain in the fifth century, the Angles. The Angles gave their name to the whole country: England is England from the Angles, not Saxonland from the Saxons; the British, the survivors of earlier populations, however, called their neighbours, often in derision, not Angle but Saxon.

The Saxons in East Anglia were mainly not of the tribe who came from Old Saxony; they were Angles from Angeln, the area now known as Schleswig-Holstein. It is clear from the pots and similar urns on the Continent that the Angles included people from the area now known as Friesland, on the North Sea coast of the Netherlands. The Frisians left their mark too in the inheritance customs of East Anglia.

East Anglia had two groups of people: the North Folk and the South Folk; the names denote the modern counties of Norfolk and Suffolk. In the centuries between the Romans and Readwald, the man most likely to have been commemorated by the great burial mound and ship burial at Sutton Hoo, deposited about A.D. 625, distinct differences grew between the two peoples. The boundary may not have been that which was later formally adopted: there is good archaeological evidence to suggest that the part of the former county of West Suffolk north of the River Lark may once have been in the territory of the North Folk. The cremation urns from Lackford, Suffolk, have close parallels with those from sites in Norfolk, particularly those found at the two cemeteries of Caistor St Edmund and Markshall, both of which are outside the Roman town of Venta Icenorum. Part of the difference lies in the rite of burial employed. Lackford is the only major cremation cemetery known in Suffolk. If one defines a major cremation cemetery as one with more than a hundred urns, Norfolk can boast a round half-dozen: Spong Hill, North Elmham, from which seven hundred urns have been published out of probably seven times that number, is the largest known cremation cemetery in England. Until 1977 that at Caistor St Edmund was the largest from which material had been most fully published. Markshall, too, has been published and that at Illington awaits the press. These are twentieth-century finds. Earlier discoveries like Castle Acre and those made in 1753 and before 1851 at Brettenham again suggest cemeteries whose size is comparable at least to the 212 urns excavated at Illington. It is not that inhumation cemeteries were absent but their grave goods, and in particular the brooches buried in the richest female graves, suggest a different alignment of cultural and trade relationships. The small site at Holkham has produced three brooches, the two most highly ornamented of which are more closely related to finds from the Midlands than from Suffolk. The most characteristic form of brooch from sixth-century Suffolk—one with an oblong upper part and a diamond-shaped foot below a ribbed bow, with each point of the diamond ending in a circular plate or lobe—does find its way into Norfolk, but significantly only to the fringes of the county. Four are known from Kenninghall, but this is only two parishes from the county boundary; the single find from Bridgham, another south Breckland parish, is similarly near the border with Suffolk. That from Brooke has passed the fire and suggests that the cemetery was not purely an inhumation one. Its occurrence may indicate a connection which took one of these brooches much further into Norfolk, to the Broadland village of Catton, just north of Norwich. That found at Hunstanton Park in 1902 must surely represent seaborne connections, as does a single East Midland brooch from the Ipswich, Hadleigh Road, cemetery.

There is another approach to the study of the Saxon settlement of an area; this is the onomatological one. Place-names have become more fashionable as indicators of settlement in the earliest centuries of Anglo-Saxon England. A chronology has been more firmly established of late. This has looked at three forms of name and suggests that the earliest is those ending in "-ham"; those ending in "-ingaham" are transitional; while those ending in "-ingas", or containing an "-inga-" element, are the latest. Unfortunately the English Place Name Society has not yet tackled Norfolk and no nineteenth-century philologist looked at the county although a rarely found Canadian study did appear in 1934. The student of the earliest English settlement whose expertise is archaeological rather than in the field of place-names must therefore rely on general books and articles when looking at Norfolk. Fortunately Norfolk was among the counties examined by Barrie Cox in his study of names in the Midlands and East Anglia published by the English Place Name Society in 1973.

Place-names, however, cannot be used apart from archaeological evidence. Those ending in "-ham", of which Bridgham is a good example, include many which are also the parishes in which early cemeteries have been found. A recent book, *Anglo-Saxon Pottery*, showed all the surviving pots from the Shropham site on a single page. With one exception all are fifth-century urns. Other "-ham" names where fifth-century urns have been found include North Elmham and Brettenham, already mentioned. The "-ingaham" names include Great Walsingham, where Sir Thomas Browne in 1658 found the "sad sepulchral pitchers" which are the earliest recorded discovery of Anglo-Saxon cinerary urns in England. A sixth-century cemetery already quoted is that from Kenninghall; the name has the element "-inga-". No fifth-century material has survived from the site.

Norfolk has no fewer than seventy "-ham" names and another seven places may possibly retain the element in their nomenclature. The probably slightly later "-ingaham" is only a little less prevalent: forty-eight are known. The two earliest forms have thus about 125 instances, almost a sixth of the county. The later "-ingas" and "-inga-" names are much fewer: only thirty-one are known.

There is a stratum of names earlier than any of these three: those derived from the presence of a walled place, a "chester". Norfolk was rural in Roman times but it did have the town of Venta Icenorum. This became Caistor, which received the epithet "St Edmund" to distinguish it from another walled town, of less importance, situated on the extreme east coast of Norfolk. The latter became Caister-on-Sea, also called Caistor-next-to-Yarmouth. The other is sometimes called Caistor-by-Norwich. The Roman defences of Britain included forts on the east coast called "the forts of the Saxon shore"; Brancaster on the north coast of the county is one. The Roman name was "Branodunum". Another of these forts was "Gariannonum", now called Burgh Castle (pronounced Borough Castle), which was among the parishes transferred to Norfolk in 1974.

Almost nine hundred years before, a division took place in England which had the most profound impact not just at the time but continuing to the present day. In 885 or 886, Alfred, king of the West Saxons, made a treaty with Guthrum, leader of the Danes, dividing the kingdom between them. The frontier ran in a line approximately due north-west from London: north and east of the line was ceded to Danish settlement. The settlement had already begun. Norfolk was the third county to be made Danish: Yorkshire in 875, Lincolnshire in 876, and our county in

879. Place-names are the best evidence of the settlement by men who spoke a language akin to Old English, intelligible to their new neighbours, and whose impact enriched the nation.

Enrichment came in a number of ways. Danes settled where no Angle had been. The Fleggs in particular have many place-names deriving from the influx of the ninth century. The suffix the new-comers gave their places was "-by", meaning a village, at least by the time these settlements were made; initially it could also mean a farm. Hemsby, Ormesby, Scratby, Filby, Mautby, all attest their presence; and again Stokesby, Herringby, Clippesby, Ashby, Oby, Rollesby, from the Fleggs. No one has yet explained the remarkable concentration of a particular form of Scandinavian place-name.

The other Scandinavian suffix, "-thorpe", is more widespread in Norfolk. It denotes an outlying and dependent settlement. Haddiscoe and Thorpe-next-Haddiscoe is an obvious example but "-thorpe" is much more common when combined with a personal name, as for example at Bagthorpe, West Norfolk, which derives from the Old Danish "Bakki". In contrast to "-by", the use of "-thorpe" is not confined to a single compact area. The only "-by" names not on the Fleggs are Alby and Colby, far away in North Norfolk, and three very close to the hinterland of Great Yarmouth: Ashby St Mary, a very small parish separated by Carleton St Peter from the River Yare, and two Kirbys. Kirby Bredon is on the Yare but Kirby Cane is inland and along the River Waveney. The modern parish includes the small settlement of that name beside the hall and the church, whose tower is Saxon, another called Kirby Green and a third, the most populous of the three at Kirby Row, much nearer the river. Aldeby, again high above the Waveney, might be thought to be another "-by" name, but in Domesday Book it is Aldborough. English not Danish is the origin of its name but the area is one of heavy Scandinavian infiltration. Toft Monks is Danish, from a word for the site of a house or homestead; it gained the epithet from a small Benedictine priory founded in the twelfth century.

Away from the extreme east of the county, the Danes gave names ending in "-thorpe" to their new villages more often but these were subsidiary settlements. The earlier discussion of Saxon cemeteries mentioned a burial ground with various names including Pensthorpe. Today it is only a farm. There are other similar names near Fakenham: Alethorpe, Thorpland, Sculthorpe, and Bagthorpe already mentioned. The area has other names of Scandinavian descent: Toftrees and Colkirk, Horningtoft and Helhoughton. Out on Norfolk's west coast there is Ingoldisthorpe, filling a space between Snettisham and Dersingham, while to the north is Holme-next-the-sea, whose first element denotes an island or dry land in the fen. The situation could not be more apt for the bleak place where west meets north on the Norfolk coast. Beside the River Great Ouse is Runcton Holme, while the subsidiary settlement denoted by "-thorpe" is aptly illustrated by the nearby Shouldham Thorpe. There is a much more populous and, in terms of its name, older settlement of Shouldham less than two kilometres distant.

The concentration of "-thorpe" names in the Tas Valley points to heavy Scandinavian settlement south of Norwich. Ashwellthorpe, Swainsthorpe and Morningthorpe are all now villages, Saxlingham Thorpe is one of the daughter settlements of Saxlingham Nethergate; it is two kilometres distant to the west while Saxlingham Green is the same distance to the east. There are other indications of the Scandinavians here. Some names are hybrid, using the English suffix "-tun" with a Danish or Norwegian personal name. One in the Tas Valley is Aslacton from "Aslakr"; Tacolneston is Danish too. One name, however, is Norwegian: Scole comes from a word meaning a temporary hut or shed.

Surviving evidence of the earliest centuries of Norfolk villages is limited. Dane and Saxon held sway a thousand years and more ago. No house standing is that old and archaeological excavation has been limited to four sunken floored structures, technically known as *grubenhauser* at Witton, near North Walsham, associated with what seems probably the vestigial remains of an animal pen. The sunken hut is difficult to interpret: uses have been suggested as diverse as weaving, on the evidence of loom-weights, storage, and general living. One at Witton was presumably used for weaving as a row of loom-weights was found and one had a hearth. The remains of the burials of the dead rather than the evidence of the houses of the living have interested students of the fifth to seventh centuries.

In contrast, from the seventh to the tenth centuries Viking burials in Eastern England can be numbered on the fingers of one hand. One of the best attested of these was found at Santon Downham, on the River Little Ouse, in 1867. There is a ninth-century sword, of a type common in Norway but with English decoration: the blade is pattern-welded. With the burial too were a pair of brooches, the most common type of the first half of the tenth century in Norway, the tortoise brooch. Other Viking swords, single finds, are known from Mileham and from Gooderstone: both are in Norwich Museum; the Santon Downham brooches and sword are in the British Museum. Viking too are the stirrups from Reffley Ferry, once a village but now within the bounds of King's Lynn, and from Kilverstone, Breckland. The one at Kilverstone was dredged from the River Thet and is now in Norwich Castle Museum; the other stirrup, again of ninth- or tenth-century date, is in King's Lynn Museum.

These few weapons do not compare with the most striking survival of the pre-Norman age in Norfolk villages. These are the Saxon churches of the county. The definitive study, *Anglo-Saxon Architecture* by H. M. and J. Taylor, lists forty-six villages with churches whose fabric certainly includes work of pre-Romanesque style; ten more have been listed as doubtful and one as improbable. Only Lincolnshire has Saxon architecture in comparable numbers. Obviously more survives at some churches than at others of the earliest period of stone construction. At Framlingham Earl, South Norfolk, only the east wall of the chancel has been rebuilt. The church was over-restored at about the same time as its contemporary at Framlingham Pigot, only two kilometres to the north, was pulled down in 1859. It was felt the Saxon structure was "a mere barn, uglier than the meanest conventicle"; the replacement was at the expense of the local landowner. The benefactor destroyed a complete late-Saxon church, consisting only of a nave and a chancel. At the other extreme the evidence can be as little as at Swainsthorpe, also in South Norfolk, where the only reliable Saxon work is a blocked south window to the nave.

The churches mentioned have been in villages in the eastern part of South Norfolk. Others here include the two churches at Haddiscoe and those at Hales, Kirby Cane, Howe, Morningthorpe, Tasburgh, Forncett St Peter, Aslacton and Gissing. This group extends into the north-east corner of Suffolk: Herringfleet, Flixton and the very early ruins at South Elmham. The latter have been suggested as the site of the cathedral of Elmham, the diocesan seat for the East Angles from 673 to the eleventh century. However, it is more probable that this was at North Elmham, in the northern part of Breckland, and now a village with a ruined church of the first half of the eleventh century built on earlier, probably late seventh-century, foundations. It is to the east of the other major concentration of Saxon churches surviving in Norfolk: those of West Norfolk and parishes on that district's eastern fringe. These include Newton-by-Castle Acre, Great Dunham, Gayton Thorpe and East Lexham, all comparatively close together, and another group of Burnham Deepdale, West Barsham, Little Snoring, Shereford and Great Ryburgh. There are others. Apart from a tower at North Walsham, there are nine surviving Saxon structures in the North Norfolk district including Thornage, Letheringsett and Weybourne, Wickmere, Bessingham and Roughton; at the last the round west tower and adjacent west wall of the nave is the earliest feature. Towers in fact are the commonest surviving Saxon work: Beechamwell, West Norfolk, has tower, nave and chancel; Beeston, in Ashamhaugh parish, North Norfolk, has a round west tower and part of the nave surviving from the Saxon church; Bessingham, North Norfolk, has a very fine west tower; the same may be said of Burnham Deepdale, West Norfolk, but West Barsham, on the extreme western edge of North Norfolk, has no surviving tower. The nave and chancel are almost completely Saxon work but a drawing by R. Ladbrooke in 1823 included in *Views of the Churches in Norfolk*, suggests a former central tower above the west end of the chancel. Another tower survives at Quidenham, Breckland, but Rockland All Saints has a surviving nave and the chancel is probably Saxon also. Saxon churches in Broadland include Heigham and Coltishall.

Sometimes only a small feature from the Saxon church survives. An example is the church of St Peter at Guestwick, on the northern fringe of Broadland. The only surviving piece of Saxon work is a tower, now most oddly positioned at the outer north-west corner of the chancel. Once there was a church with a nave, central tower and chancel, rather as at Newton-by-Castle Acre, Breckland. At Guestwick the nave has been replaced and moved to the south and the chancel completely destroyed. The result is an irregularly planned church mostly in the Perpendicular style of the fifteenth century, retaining the Saxon tower. The nave has aisles and a long chancel; the tower once served as a north transept: it is topped with a fifteenth-century belfry stage.

Occasionally Saxon churches are mentioned in contemporary documents but references are rare. Great Melton had two churches from before 1000 when land was bequeathed to a church, probably that of All Saints' which survives in use. It and St Mary's were both in use with separate livings until 1713 but a century later All Saints' was partly ruined. However, by 1883 the position was reversed and St Mary's had been pulled down and the partially ruined All Saints' rebuilt. As early as 1849 a Norfolk architectural writer, John Gunn, who was vicar of Irstead until 1875, commented on the Saxon date of All Saints' because the nave had a double-splayed window, one where both the inner and outer faces of the wall are cut back to take the window. This seems to have been a casualty of the 1883 rebuilding but positive evidence of the date of the nave, from a straight joint (itself indicating a change in building date between two portions of walling which are not bonded together) a third of the way along the north side, is provided by a blocked north doorway. The head has tiles set in a non-radial fashion in the manner of those of the church at Treddington, Warwickshire, and the door jambs have no imposts, being of flint with only isolated tiles as bonding. The south-east quoin of the nave is also Saxon work; the chancel quoins although heavily restored seem also to be of a similar age. These corners are of flint and tile; the quoining was also noted in 1849 by John Gunn. Other standing churches he suggested as early are those at Witton, Weybourne, Framlingham Earl, Coltishall and Colney. Of these Framlingham Earl is particularly important as it is among the fifty-five churches which give primary evidence for the dating of Anglo-Saxon architectural features. The church has been noted as an almost complete survival from before the Norman Conquest. Only the porches and the present squared east end are later. But it is in the details that the dating evidence is found: both north and south doorways are of plain round-headed form, cut straight through the wall and made without dressed stone facings. Into these openings Norman stone door-frames have been inserted. Dressed stone has not been used for the quoins of the nave, all four of which have large flints in the lower parts and smaller flints above. Flints too have been used for the chancel pilasters, which originally designated the beginning of an apsidal east end: the feature is a unique survival. Surviving Saxon windows at Framlingham Earl are limited to two small double-splayed circular openings a metre from the junction of nave and chancel and a metre from the top of the chancel wall. Neither was originally glazed: Birds were excluded by means of a string gauze mounted on a wooden frame. One was found here; a similar example is known at another village in Norfolk, South Lopham.

It would be possible to write a book devoted entirely to the Saxon churches of Norfolk. At one church the striking feature belongs to a later century. In *The Buildings of England: North-West and South Norfolk*, Sir Nikolaus Pevsner placed the tower of St Andrew's, South Lopham, at no later than 1120. It stands between a fourteenth-century chancel and a fifteenth-century nave with adjacent south aisle and south porch. Yet this arresting tower, of five stages with typical Norman windows, and later battlements, is not the earliest record of a church at South Lopham. Neither, too, is a blocked doorway on the north wall of the aisle, for above this is a single circular double-splayed window, of Saxon date. South Lopham church was large even before the Norman Conquest. Usually in a general survey such as *Norfolk Villages*, precise details of the size of churches would be out of place. However, the nave of South Lopham church is 13·42 metres (44 feet) long and 5·92 metres (19 feet 5 inches) wide: the nave at Framlingham Earl is shorter, only 9·15 metres (30 feet) long on the south side and a little more on the north, and narrower, a mere 5·18 metres (17 feet) wide. The latter is about a metre less than the average length.

Given the large choice, and there are more villages in Norfolk with a Saxon church than in any other county, some further selection has to be exercised. The former parish church at Weybourne, North Norfolk, is twelfth century but incorporates a pre-Conquest parish church. The priory is now a ruin; the present church uses only the south aisle of the priory as a nave. This was the post-Dissolution church, to which a north aisle was added in 1866 on the site of the former Saxon nave. Weybourne tower was therefore an axial one: an original chancel occupies the crossing space of the medieval priory: a large early fourteenth-century arch has been cut into the Saxon tower. This has only its southern half surviving; enough, however, to indicate its elaborate decoration.

The lower stage was plain but at the belfry stage there was a double window on each of the four faces with twin triangular-headed openings and the wall spaces had flat stripwork in flint; above were two circular, double-splayed openings, more probably sound-holes rather than windows: four of the eight survive.

Many of the churches of Norfolk are ruined: a count done during the Second World War noted 659 churches in use dating to before 1700 and another 245 ruined churches. Ruined Saxon churches include two with axial towers: Castle Rising Chapel and St James's at Bawsey. The extent of the desertion discussed in our next chapter is shown here: another church, of Norman date from its earliest reported features, dedicated to St Michael, is also in ruins. Great Dunham, West Norfolk, like Great Melton, once had two churches: one is now covered by the rectory garden and may have been more fine than the existing one. Dedications are difficult to sort out: St Mary and St Andrew were the respective dedicatees but which was originally appended to the surviving church is not clear. Like Framlingham Earl the chancel at Great Dunham was originally apsidal at the east end and, as has been supposed for the South Norfolk church, this too was one with an original west entrance. A fine gable-headed western doorway survives, now blocked. One is reminded of the details, more lavish it is true, of Barton-on-Humber, South Humberside (formerly Lincolnshire), and those of Earl's Barton, Northamptonshire; the dating is similar, the middle and later years of the eleventh century for the upper part of the tower of Barton-on-Humber. The rest of this structure and the tower at Earl's Barton are a century or so earlier. Pilaster strips as decoration were less common on later Saxon structures. The plain towers of both Great Dunham and Newton-by-Castle Acre suggest this. Both have two-light belfry windows: at Great Dunham above a single, double-splayed window on the second stage, that above the nave height. Great Dunham has blank arcading inside the nave: eight bays on the north wall, one more on the south, but with the four at the eastern end occupying the same length as three on the north side. Here they are all of the same width: 1·2 metres (3 feet 11 inches) for the recess and 330 millimetres (16½ inches) for the strips.

Actually in Breckland is Newton-by-Castle Acre: Castle Acre is on the eastern edge of West Norfolk. It presents an immediate contrast to Great Dunham. The latter has the tower as a continuation of the nave; at Newton the tower is the western part of the chancel. Another contrast is that Newton once had a south chapel, or porticus: a north one has also been claimed. The positive evidence is a blocked doorway with a later lancet window on the south side of the lower stage of the tower; rough walling can also be seen indicating the west wall of the porticus and the roof-join.

At the other end of the county are the remaining churches to be discussed in this chapter. But first a brief mention must be made of Roughton, North Norfolk, basically an early fourteenth-century church with a tall, narrow, round tower, of pre-Conquest appearance. The tower at Great Ryburgh, too, may be of this age, at least in the stages below the belfry: the rest of the large, aisle-less church is basically fourteenth century. St Mary's, Tasburgh, is another church whose tower dates to around the time of the Norman Conquest: style in architecture is often unrelated to political history. The Saxon date of Tasburgh tower is shown by the series of seven blind arcades on the external face of the tower at the level of the nave roof: the western one with a round-headed window and windows also in the two central pilasters to north and south. Another arcade above this has been cut away at the top to allow for a later medieval rebuilding with four belfry openings, pointed and wider than the Saxon windows. The tower arch at Tasburgh is tall: no less than 5·16 metres (16 feet 11 inches) high when built.

Blind arcading recurs elsewhere in Norfolk. St Matthias's at Haddiscoe Thorpe is an attractive church: thatched roof to a flint-built nave, with a later brick and tiled chancel, and a round tower. The original church was without the tower: high in the west wall of the nave is a round window, double-splayed and now blocked by the tower. As at Framlingham Earl, two cells, a nave and a chancel were all that was originally built. To this was added a tower of which the third stage was provided with a blind arcade. This is now cut away to provide for a Norman belfry. There is much that is Norman at Haddiscoe Thorpe. St Matthias's Church has doorways and a big square font. A later feature, probably thirteenth-century, is a pair of pointed arches forming a double recess in the west wall of the nave; their function is uncertain but an alms cupboard has been suggested.

Within three kilometres of Haddiscoe Thorpe and on the main road from Great Yarmouth to Scole, Diss and Bury St Edmunds —the modern A143 eventually ends in Haverhill, in the south-west corner of Suffolk—is Haddiscoe; a road from here goes to Beccles, which means that earlier the road is called "Beccles Road" in Gorleston and Bradwell. Haddiscoe, too, has a Saxon tower to its church. St Mary's has a massive ground stage, some 7 or 8 metres high (around 25 feet), taller than the two next stages. Each of these has a round-headed window on each of the three external faces resting on a string course. Above is a set of four double belfry openings, with triangular heads and cylindrical shafts. A church with double belfry openings with gabled hoods is St Mary's, Bessingham. Both churches are provided with tall tower arches of the usual round-headed type. Both have another doorway into the tower at a much higher stage than the tall tower arch. At Bessingham it is triangular-headed while that at Haddiscoe is round-headed.

This survey has concentrated on what might be described as the archaeologically interesting Saxon churches of Norfolk villages. Indeed of Haddiscoe it has been written: "altogether the church presents a fascinating combination of Anglo-Saxon and Norman features, well worthy of further detailed study." Another church equally fascinating is that at Hales. Externally Romanesque, attractive with its thatched roof and aspidal-ended chancel to a simple aisleless nave and round-towered church, remote from the village it serves, St Margaret's Church, Hales, seems to belong to the period after the final Viking onslaught. The Norman Conquest was an event more devastating, more destructive and more vicious than the Danish settlement of Norfolk in 879. Normandy is the land of the north men; in a sense its architecture breathed a more cosmopolitan air than the insular creations of Saxon masons. The Saxons are men not to be despised. Hales is a good example of their work and their working methods. Within the round west tower are two double-splayed circular windows, one to the north, one to the south. Impressed in the internal splays of each is the basket-work construction upon which the Saxon masons built their arch of rubble and mortar. Their work has stood the test of time, a thousand years perhaps or a little less—in such dimensions a century is mere portion.

It could be objected, because of the paucity of evidence and the difficulties of interpretation, that the earliest time of Norfolk villages is too meagre for lengthy discussion. But when the Norman conquerors came, in 1066 and the years beyond, Norfolk villages were already as many generations old as were to pass before the Tudors sat on the throne the Vikings usurped. The diocese too was almost as old. Founded at North Elmham in 673, it survived in this Norfolk village to 1077. Covering all of Norfolk and much of Suffolk, the see was at Thetford for only seventeen years. From 1094 onwards Norfolk villages were within the diocese of Norwich. Yet of those villages—eight hundred is a round figure—there is evidence surviving still of the piety of men before 1094 in no less than forty-six. Like the place-names bequeathed by the earliest inhabitants—Saxon and Dane alike—it is striking evidence of the depth of history present in the villages of Norfolk.

II

Expansion and Decline: Domesday and Deserted Villages

MANY churches of pre-Conquest date, reflecting the heavy settlement of the area, survive in Norfolk. The Conqueror came and, like all victors, needed to take stock of the land he had taken. The result in 1086 was the compilation of a great manuscript, Domesday Book. It gives a picture of an eleventh-century society covering a whole country; from this unique record individual villages and lands can be examined. It is not complete: no record ever is; churches in particular are badly listed by the men who surveyed Norfolk and its villages. Only 217 are noted, in 731 settlements other than the three boroughs, Thetford, Norwich and Yarmouth. Norfolk is big: the fourth in size of the traditional counties of England, but its population today is small for the area. In 1086 it was big. A computation has given a population figure for the whole of England as listed in Domesday Book as 268,984 but these are heads of households only. A million is the usually accepted figure for the whole country. For Norfolk, the figure was 26,309; so 100,000 would seem a reasonable working estimate of the population of the county. In any but the most precise calculations, which themselves are open to wide statistical deviations, one may assume that a tenth of England's population lived in Norfolk and its villages. No other county approached its numbers, although six others had a figure of over 10,000. The two next most populous were the adjacent counties of Lincolnshire and Suffolk.

The people of Norfolk villages in 1086 lived in settlements of widely varying size and under as many as a dozen lords in the largest places or a single lord as at Bircham Newton, West Norfolk. No two of the rural settlements were alike. A general book on Norfolk villages must be selective; some general observations may be in order. Domesday Book is not a record primarily of villages; it is a record of land-holdings and land ownership. The unit of land-holding in the eleventh century and beyond was the manor, and though manor and village may be the same, more often they are not. Forncett St Mary and Costessey are villages now; in 1086 they were manors with portions in other villages for their land. Of the manor of Costessey in Forehoe Hundred, portions lay elsewhere in the same hundred (as a Saxon administrative district was called): at Honingham, at Brandon Parva, at Runhall and at Carleton Forehoe and probably also in its detached portions, the berewicks, at Bawburgh and Honingham Thorpe as well as at Easton, Marlingford, Barford and Wramplingham. There are lost settlements too: "Toketorp" and "Appetorp", both in Forehoe Hundred. But Costessey manor went beyond its own hundred, to East Tuddenham and Yaxham in Midford Hundred, Weston Longueville in Eynesford Hundred and Attlebridge and Felthorpe in Taverham Hundred, a ring of places in hundreds to the west and north of Costessey. Norwich is to the east, but south, a whole hundred away, is Depwade Hundred. Here settlements abound with lands part of the manor of Costessey in the fief of Earl Alan: Tibenham, Aslacton, Moulton St Michael, Wacton and Morningthorpe, Carleton Rode, Kettleton, Middleton, Swanton and Tasburgh were part of the berewick of Long Stratton, with Flordon over the boundary in Humbleyard Hundred. Some of these villages were part also of Forncett manor, based on Forncett St Mary. Forncett St Peter, with its fine Saxon church tower, was then called Twanton, and was part of the lands of Roger Bigod. His lands, and those of men who rented from him, extended both in 1086 and in 1565, when another survey was taken, into Aslacton, Wacton, Moulton St Michael, Tibenham, Carleton Rode, Long Stratton and Tasburgh of the villages mentioned before. The lands were also in other villages: Tacolneston, Tharston, Shelton, Fritton, Fundenhall and Hapton. At Shelton and at Moulton St Michael, new manors developed; in 1086, they had both direct tenants of Roger Bigod and sub-tenants. Elsewhere there was the tendency to create new manors from old holdings which rendered some small service to the original manor. At Aslacton, this seems to have been the case.

The structure of society in the eleventh century is apparent from Domesday Book in a way that is not clear in such depth until the Elizabethan years, when visitations, tax returns and parish registers make individuals in villages come alive. The status of men changed with the advent of the Normans. In 1066 most peasant farmers who were unfree worked for their lords as villeins, but thereafter their freedom declined and they acquired the lower position of bordars (in which they were required to work harder for their lord). For example, records show that at Newton-by-Castle Acre the 8 villeins and 7 bordars in 1066 had become 2 villeins and 11 bordars in 1086. At Kerdiston the 30 villeins in 1066 had become 16 villeins and 14 bordars in 1086. At Methwold the 4 bordars had increased to 13 in 1086, and there were 10 fewer villeins by then. Compared with this diminution of status of the unfree, everywhere the number of slaves was either constant or declining, whilst the number of freemen and sokemen (who possessed rights within their 'soke' or district) seems not to have declined and sometimes increased between the Conquest and the Domesday inquest, for example at Barnham Broom, Kimberley and Welborne.

There were other diminutions too, more subtle than population loss, more complete than the loss of status. Conquest is never easily absorbed, and upon England the Norman barons wrought a terrible revenge for the display of audacious courage, for the refusal to comply with the brutal land-grabbing the Conquest inflicted. Men who speak Old English (like those who speak the twentieth-century dialect derived therefrom) do not like the ways, perhaps more sophisticated but certainly more effete, of vultures in London and men imposed from other lands. Only with the harshness of Normandy, if he had known it, could the ordinary Norfolk villager have sympathized in 1066.

The villages of Norfolk felt the pillage of the Conquest at an early date. It was not the change in ownership which affected the lives of the majority of people. Although 379 manors came into Norman hands, the significant and destructive effect was in the woodland of the county. Launditch Hundred, in the northern part of modern Breckland, has four examples of a reduction in woodland between 1066 and 1086. At three villages—North Elmham,

Mileham and the lost Suttona—the quantity halved, while at Gateley the quantity of woodland would support only a quarter of the number of pigs compared with twenty years earlier. The same goes for Broadland: both Horsham and Horsford in Taverham Hundred show woodland to support half the number of pigs in 1086 as had been possible in 1066.

Upon the ordinary villages of the eleventh century it is possible to argue that the much-vaunted Conquest had little effect. They continued to plough the fields as they had done before the change in kingship. They still worshipped in the same churches. Proof of this is the many Saxon churches surviving.

There were changes of course in the churches but, as J. Romilly Allen pointed out in the *Victoria County History of Norfolk* as long ago as 1906, the architectural sculpture which is much-praised often owes as much to the Saxon mason as to the Norman patron. The men of action are more to be praised than those who merely accrue profits from other men's labours without themselves making a substantial investment. Haddiscoe has featured already in this book. The effigy in St Mary's Church deserves to be better known; the seated figure within a richly carved surround has been variously interpreted as a Christ in Majesty and as Pope Gregory I. The sculpture occupies a niche above the Norman south door: the north one is Norman too. Tympana with figures are rare in Norfolk. Two only are known, both in West Norfolk, but the one at St Michael's, Mintlyn, is choked in nettles, and that at St Botolph's, Tottenhill, is essentially a cross with rope-moulding.

More striking are the fonts of Norman date in village churches. Three have figurative carvings, but only two of these use this style on all four sides. The subjects vary. Twelve men are shown on the four sides of the font at St Mary's, Burnham Deepdale, West Norfolk. They are the labours of the months. A year's cycle is shown. In January the man has a drinking horn. In February he is warming his feet: winter was always cruel, and craftsmen in stone understood their neighbours' afflictions. In March, the work of providing the food began with digging; in April it was pruning but in May men took time off to beat the bounds of their parish. It is a custom found much later than 1100. Without maps no village could know its own lands except by walking their periphery. In June there was weeding and in July scything. A sheaf was bound in August and corn threshed in September. It was ground on a quern in October. Baking is not shown but a beast was slaughtered in November for the feasting in mid-winter. December's topic on Burnham Deepdale font, like its eleven companions, has as much and as little to do with Christian imagery since it refers to ageless customs of an agricultural world. Burnham Deepdale is the village most westerly of the Norfolk Burnhams and is now in Brancaster parish. At St Martin's, Fincham, the font came from the now destroyed St Michael's Church. Three scenes reflect the earliest events of the New Testament—the Nativity, the Adoration of the Magi and the Baptism of Christ—but one shows the temptation of Adam and Eve. Over the district boundary in North Norfolk is All Saints', Sculthorpe, where only one face of the font has a figurative scene: the east has an Adoration of the Magi. But the glory of this font is the powerful interlace on the south face. The Saxon carved this as surely as he contributed his skill to the knot patterns of the font at All Saints', Toftrees, and that at St Andrew's, Little Snoring. His vigour can even be seen on the font on four small columns in the village church of St Peter and St Paul, Shernborne, again in West Norfolk. Much of the best eleventh- and twelfth-century work is to be found in villages in this district and just to the east.

The Norman contribution to Norfolk villages is more than isolated examples of architectural sculpture. In some villages a whole church was provided: Heckingham is a good example, Hales another. The south doorway of St Gregory's, Heckingham, South Norfolk, has four orders of shaft each with decorated capitals, and an arch with the usual Romanesque range of zig-zag and other motifs. The same craftsman is thought to have made the north doorway of St Margaret's, Hales, also in South Norfolk. This church has been mentioned in Chapter I on account of its Saxon window; Norman and fine are the chancel and apse with buttresses and once-continuous arcading.

The small is impressive; the large more grand than anything. The late, non-Domesday marshland villages of Norfolk include Tilney All Saints, where the sizeable church has a late Norman arcade of seven bays, encompassing both nave and chancel. This is a century later than Domesday. The marsh in the Fenland part of West Norfolk was heavily colonized in the twelfth century. Another grand design of this century is All Saints', Walsoken, huge in its concept: seven bays of nave and another two of chancel, all in that solid style the Normans brought to their England.

Solidity: it sums up the Norman influence on Norfolk villages. The churches show some of it. Villages have no domestic architecture that old, but there are castles. Stone was rarely used for castles outside of towns, but Castle Rising in Norfolk is an exception. William d'Albini, who built it, died in 1176. There are extensive earthworks, within which is a fragment of stone-walling with herringbone masonry, part of the chapel, built a century before the great keep. This keep is rivalled only by that at Norwich. It is broader than it is high, with the main floor at the second stage. Men have climbed for eight hundred years up the impressive steps on the east side. The ground floor, reached by an internal newel stair, was used for storage and is partly vaulted. The main hall, whose portal was converted into a fireplace with Bawsey tiles in the sixteenth century, occupied the northern quarter of the keep, full length along one side; the remainder served as a gallery with a chapel attached. The village also has Norman building in its church. The west front of St Lawrence's Church has been described as a "swagger piece of Norman decoration", such is its exuberance. The tower too is Norman, although with a restored top of 1844, when much was done and "details not previously apparent exposed".

There is a sense in which Castle Rising is a decayed town. A hackneyed rhyme recalls:

Rising was a sea-port
When Lynn was but a marsh,
Now Lynn it is the sea-port
And Rising fares the worse.

Long before 1832, the town had ceased to justify its inclusion in the boroughs which sent members to Parliament: representatives had included Samuel Pepys, the London diarist of the seventeenth century, and Horace Walpole, the eighteenth-century *littérateur* who did at least have Norfolk ancestors and lived in the county.

Another village with a twelfth-century keep, also in West Norfolk, is Weeting. The castle has a main range of a hall and flanking works. The hall was keep-like and of three storeys. Earthworks were more commonly used to dominate: Weeting, Wormgay and Mileham are run of the mill, but Castle Acre is "perhaps the finest castle earthworks in England". The village has also the extensive remains of the Cluniac priory, founded by William de Warenne in 1090. That was Norman with a vengeance and in plan recalls the second building at the order's first house, Cluny, in France: nave with aisles, and two towers at the west end, a proper crossing tower, transepts with apsidal chapels and chancel with aisles all terminating in apses. The ruin is magnificent in its display: the tiered arcades on the west front, dating to the 1140s and the last thing to be built of the basic plan, impress with their symmetry, broken only by the fifteenth-century window, replacing earlier provision. Of the monastic church only one bay on the south side is well preserved: testimony to the destructive force lavished on the monasteries in the wake of Henry VIII's whirlwind. Claustral buildings surviving at Castle Acre include both dormitory and reredorter as well as two halls of the infirmary, one of which is Norman, the other belongs to the early fourteenth century. By then the castle which gave its name to the place was the group of mounds and walls we see today. The earthworks cover six hectares (fifteen acres). Dominating them is a mound of earth, a motte of great height: over 30 metres (100 feet) from the bottom of the ditch to the top. The earthworks are so large they encompass the whole village. A gatehouse with two round towers of the thirteenth century remains on the way into the village from the green. The south gate, however, was demolished by the Victorians. The castle's buildings have been much robbed, to be used as building stone, but from the road east of Castle Acre a good view can be had, showing how the stone buildings and the curtain walls sit in relation to the earthworks. A massive keep remains.

Looking at Castle Acre—castle, monastic remains, both church and claustral buildings, and even the parish church—we realize the distance we are from the England which fathered them. Men are still ruthless in their greed, avaricious in their quest to dominate others; the monuments they erect may not be castles of stone and earth, but the basic fear which made the Normans dominate Norfolk and all of England with their creations remains in men who have amassed more than their fair share of this world's goods. Men still need the strength of religious belief, and those who seek to give often seek something in return, a form of spiritual prestige which has little to do with religious feeling.

Religious feeling there was in abundance in medieval Norfolk and its villages. Take Binham St Mary with its arcaded front of before 1244, probably the first to be built in the Early English style. Richard de Parco, abbot of this Benedictine priory from 1226 to his death, is credited with the work. The priory survives because the village would have had no parish church after 1536 had not the Norman nave been used, deprived of the aisles and with late Perpendicular style windows within the lowest tier of the three-storey arcades.

Binham Priory was established in 1091 and has extensive remains. Yet of Lessingham Priory, founded a year before, nothing now remains. Other monastic remains have had varying fates. Of Hickling Priory, founded 1185, there is a solid wall in a field and some cloister arcading but nothing of the church. From Broomholm Priory, founded in 1113, there survives a two-storey north transept—a most odd fragment indeed—an unroofed chapter house, parts of the main claustral buildings, and a gatehouse. There is a solitary tower and the gatehouse left at West Acre Priory, founded about 1100, and of Creake Abbey, founded in 1206, parts of the crossing from the church stand gaunt against the sky. Of a later foundation, Burnham Norton Friary of 1241, enlarged in 1353, there is a gatehouse and parts of a chapel together with isolated fragments incorporated into other buildings.

The destruction which the Reformation wrought is aptly brought out by the monastic houses of Norfolk. Of the thirty houses in 1535, only two had massive incomes: Walsingham and St Benet's at Holme, Ludham. The demolition of St Benet's was total. Only the gatehouse remains, much painted by J. S. Cotman and by John Crome among others of the Norwich school of landscape painters in the nineteenth century. There are also a few meagre walls from the church. Whereas the four monastic establishments of the Nar valley—Castle Acre, West Acre, Pentney and Blackborough (or Wormegay)—are pleasantly sited, St Benet's is bleak; even on a mild and sunny day, it is best left to the farmer's cows who inhabit the site today.

The sense of desolate distance from the world, inspired by St Benet's, may have been intentional. The monastic ideal involved a withdrawal from the world. For the ordinary villagers, the parish church was their centre. Norfolk villages are rich in parish churches, and in the early Middle Ages became even more richly endowed still as new villages were founded and settlements split into separate communities, each with their own church.

Norfolk already had many villages at the time of the Conquerors' inquest. Yet the process of creating new villages went on. Often these were the first to be abandoned. Regression was as much a part of early medieval village settlement as expansion. Part of the expansion was measured in villages with the same name. New villages on the marsh began as one Terrington, one Tilney, one Walpole, one Wiggenhall. Today the first and the third comprise two settlements distinguished by the name of the patron saint of their parish church. There are now three Tilneys and four Wiggenhalls. There is a Wiggenhall St Germans, a Wiggenhall St Mary the Virgin, a Wiggenhall St Mary Magdalen and a Wiggenhall St Peter; the area of the last-named is now included in the third.

Elsewhere in the county the new villages did not survive the Middle Ages. Shotesham today is a single civil parish. In 1845 there were two but the process of reduction was then only half completed. As William White's *Directory* in 1845 noted of Low Shotesham, it comprised "the consolidated parishes of Shotesham St Mary, St Martin, and St Botolph". But, even in 1726 when Francis Bloomfield, the Norfolk historian, wrote these were annexed to High Shotesham or Shotesham All Saints. White noted of the churches: "St Mary's Church is a small edifice in good repair; but St Martin's and St Botolph's have been in ruins for several centuries." By the twentieth century only the main village church has survived.

A village with two churches surviving in use is Rocklands, a modern creation in Breckland district: Rockland St Peter was in Wayland Hundred, Rockland All Saints and St Andrew in Shropham Hundred. The parish priest today serves both and Shropham to the south. St Andrew's Church was dilapidated when Francis Bloomfield wrote; part of the tower stands gaunt in a field, uncultivated and not deconsecrated, a solitary reminder of medieval expansion. The benefices of All Saints and St Andrew had been consolidated in 1550. Beyond Shropham is Hockham, once two parishes and with the main village still called Great Hockham. William White, echoing Bloomfield, remarked that the church of Little Hockham was not demolished until the fifteenth century; there is a reference to it in the reign of Richard II (1377–99).

In 1616 there were five tenants and two houses; those houses were there twenty-one years later and both the manor house, now a farm, and another survive.

It is quite common to find names of Norfolk villages with the same basic element. There is a North Creake and a South Creake, a North Pickenham and a South Pickenham, a Great Cressingham and a Little Cressingham, an East Winch and a West Winch with a Middleton between, and using their patron saints, a Tivetshall St Margaret and a Tivetshall St Mary. These, like the settlements on the marsh, have flourished and survive to the present day as separate villages. Others, of course, do not. Oxborough Hithe is a farm in Oxborough parish; another deserted medieval village in this parish is Caldecote, now a farm and the remains of a church. Tittleshall has two former villages within its bounds: Godwick and Gramston. Both were live settlements in 1596 when a map was made, although the second had lost many of its houses. Godwick, though, had manor house, nine other houses, the church and a mill with millpond. Not all desertion of medieval villages belongs to the centuries before 1500 and virtually none can be ascribed to the Black Death of 1348.

Of the places mentioned, Caldecote and Godwick are both exceptionally well-preserved earthworks. Other good sites are Pudding Norton and Bawsey, both of which remain as parish names although at neither is the church now more than a shell. Bawsey was one of the places where a notice of the perambulation of the bounds of Castle Rising Chace was posted in 1816; another is the adjacent Leziate and a third Appleton, near Flitcham. Yet in 1845 the last was described as "a deserted ruin, of which the dilapidated tower and walls of the nave remain" with a large elder tree in the latter "among the mutilated flagstones inscribed to the memory of the Paston family". A branch of the family lived there until 1707 when fire destroyed their mansion. Modern Bawsey had two churches in the Middle Ages; both are now in ruins. St Michael's, the church of Mintlyn, is choked in nettles; that dedicated to St James has more remaining but time is ravaging further a building which had "been a roofless ruin upwards of a century" already by 1845. Even then there was less still of the church at Leziate where in 1845 "nothing remains but the foundation". Even that has been obliterated today. Alone among the villages directly east of King's Lynn Ashwicken retains its church. An avenue of chestnuts forms the approach; the tower is the thrill, a pyramid on the roof two centuries earlier than the blue diaper-patterned decoration of the brickwork of the big west buttresses erected by a Tudor squire.

If one seeks an explanation for the desertion of Bawsey, Leziate and Glosthorpe (to the south of Ashwicken), the yards of sand extracted daily speak volumes of the unsuitability of the soil for cultivation. The sea has claimed more than one Norfolk village: Shipden, the forerunner of Cromer; Eccles, famous for the two lumps of stone on the beach, all that survives of the church; also here are Whimpwell to the north and Little Waxham to the south. Waxham itself behind Marram Hills is small enough: church, hall, barn, another farm at one site and Brograve Farm to the south. It looks like a shrunken if not a decayed or a deserted village.

Desertion of Norfolk villages is not merely medieval; there are Yorkist and Tudor depopulations caused by sheep farming, but these are few. More significant were the specific cases of emparking in the eighteenth century discussed in Chapter V. For the most part the deserted villages of Norfolk, which number no fewer than 130, are simply those places which could not grow anything—except, that is, trees. It must speak loudly of the poor quality of the soil of Breckland, for here is where the deserted medieval villages frequently are: Buckenham Tofts, Sturston, Langford, Lynford, West Wretham. It is a great blank area where modern tanks roam across the battle area of the army's practice zone. West of Thetford is Roudham and Kilverstone and few live on Brettenham Heath. Great Snarehill is another village which has gone completely; West Harling is reduced to trees, two houses and a church.

It is only the churches which survive from medieval Norfolk. They alone speak of the density of the villages now subsumed in a single civil parish. In 1971, the census recorded the population of the civil parish of Quidenham. Only 401 people were noted —that is, 114 fewer than a decade earlier. Yet in this large area, 2,250 hectares (5,560 acres), there are no fewer than four churches each denoting a former village: Hargham, Eccles, Wilby and Quidenham itself. On this basis the density of settlement is as high as in South Norfolk: Framlingham Earl and Framlingham Pigot lie cheek-by-jowl with Kirby Bredon, Bramerton, Holverston, Yelverton and Alpington and these seven comprise almost a hundred hectares less than modern Quidenham. If one conducts the same exercise on another five parishes also in South Norfolk one sees a slightly less dense settlement but again modern Quidenham is more than a hundred hectares larger. Of these five, Flordon has less than the population of Quidenham today, and Swainsthorpe is about the same. Both Newton Flotman and Swardeston have half as many people again and at Mulbarton the total is almost three times that of the bare waste of a Breckland parish. Yet men once lived in Quidenham and its surrounding villages, if not in numbers as great as in South Norfolk at least enough to build four churches.

They built three churches at East, West and North Barsham, in North Norfolk, and three at Great Bircham, Bircham Newton and Bircham Tofts, not far distant in West Norfolk. In the forty years before 1949 a Suffolk man, Henry Munro Cautley, came and wrote a book on the then surviving 659 churches and the 245 ruined ones, all dating to before 1700: Thetford had three, Yarmouth one and Norwich the staggering number of thirty-three. Market towns and villages, if we take away the three in King's Lynn as well, provide a corpus of no fewer than 864 known churches considered in *Norfolk Churches*. *Norfolk Villages* is not primarily a book about churches; it is more an evocation of the subject. Yet within that subject the church plays a significant part. Village life centred on the church in the Middle Ages far more than it does today. Even in the late twentieth century village life can be seen as requiring a centre and the Anglican church is often alone in providing that centre. The Church has had a differing role throughout the various centuries of the last millennium: architectural splendour in the Middle Ages and benefaction by individuals in the late fifteenth and early sixteenth centuries are apparent. All changed with the Reformation and the Church assumed a mantle that placed the state at the centre of a secular world. New ideas in the seventeenth century and a very different form of display in the eighteenth century did not lessen the Church's importance in the Victorian village; today it can be seen as the final bastion of an older world, not quite the condemnation of the twentieth century's hideous materialism but at least some reflection of a very different set of values.

On the North Norfolk coast, Cley-next-the-Sea, Blakeney,

Wiveton and Morston all have churches which reflect the respect, affection and care men lavished on their place of worship and which commanded their involvement. At Cley the transepts are ruined now, an echoing reminder on a bleak windswept day of the ravages time has brought to even the most prosperous of villages. The sea has receded and on the marshes, teal and tern, sandpiper and swift hold sway. Now a bird sanctuary, Cley marshes and those of Salthouse to the east belong as much to the birds as to men; cattle do graze between the road on the limit of the land and the edge of the sea. Boats no longer sail from Cley-next-the-Sea and the stark open tracery of the south transept window of St Margaret's Church is a reminder that Cley was a port that vied with Lynn and with Yarmouth. North Norfolk and its coastal harbours lost their commerce with foreign lands in the fifteenth century and after. Lacking the yachting trade of nearby Blakeney, Cley has declined to a centre for ornithology alone. The village boasts few tourists, and few new houses. It is a long way, sadly, from the thriving port; the south porch of the church marks the latter and looks out over the village green to the site of the old harbour facing Wiveton.

Wiveton church is late fourteenth century in date; a guiding light from Cley whose own edifice is hidden behind the houses of the village. Lone and isolated from its village it stands above the former harbour. Blakeney church inspires no such affection: it is stark against the road, behind and away from the quay. But at Morston where the road snakes through the village the big almost empty churchyard is home to a church built when the thirteenth century turned into the fourteenth. Yet despite the lack of graves and their stones within the rector's acres, or perhaps because of this lack, Morston is the most striking church on the coast road. The village is small but not without a sense of belonging both to the past and to the future.

III

The Splendour of Wool

In the days when a man's suit was made of woollen cloth, and not as is more often the case today of man-made fibre, the bolt from which the piece was drawn would more likely than not have been of worsted. William Paston, writer of the famous Paston letters, could ask for "two ells of worsted for doublets". It was famed long before his time, the fifteenth century. There also belongs the splendour of wool.

Wool and its weaving was the trade of a small part of Norfolk, essentially a block of villages north of Norwich and the River Wensum, west of the Broads and going no further west than East Dereham. A few weavers' villages exist south of the river, around Mattishall on the River Tud, a tributary which flows into the River Wensum at Hellesdon. The names trip off the tongue: Worstead, Cawston, Sall (or Salle) and Trunch are all memorable for the brilliance and the magnificence of their churches.

The church of St Mary, Worstead, can be seen for miles. The tower, standing 33·25 metres (109 feet) high, dominates the landscape for miles around. The guide books proclaim its building with the rest of the church in 1379. The church is huge, reflecting the earlier importance of the place: today the living is appended to that at North Walsham, such is the decline of Worstead. Vast churches need more than their size to impress and Worstead is a great disappointment. "Barren" is an adjective one would wish to apply to this barn no less complex in its conception than another over-rated tabernacle, St Nicholas's, Great Yarmouth. These two share an emptiness that defies intimacy although the coldness which can be frightening is not sensed at St Mary's, Worstead, as it is in the other.

Obviously there are good things about the church: a screen of 1512 given by John Arblaster and his wife, Agnes, is a fair example of sixteenth-century woodwork, but the churches built on the wealth of wool have better. The ringers' gallery under the tower is a decade earlier and the font cover is an example of the Perpendicular style. We shall have cause to notice others. The roof too belongs to the turn of the sixteenth century. A clerestory was not in the initial conception; the earlier roof-line is preserved against the tower. Perhaps the best thing in Worstead church is the porch, double-storeyed with a vault on the ground floor, and requiring one to turn right before entering the south door.

The village too is not much: a few flint houses with brick interspersed. One leaves Worstead disappointed and with a sense that the whole is better viewed across the fields on the low rise whereon it stands than sampled at close quarters. Tunstead to the south is much less well known but, like Sloley, the parish to the north separating it from Worstead, the now-isolated church has nice touches. To take St Mary's, Tunstead, first; like Worstead it is big and in fact three metres or so longer. The first attraction is the ironwork on the south door, a pretty design around a central boss, still used to turn the latch of this two-part door. There are benches on the aisle walls and another massive screen, vaulted and lacking the rood loft, dividing nave from chancel firmly and without equivocation. An age of participation for all in religious services finds it hard to comprehend the firm separation the late Middle Ages imposed between priest and people.

At Sloley the font in St Bartholomew's Church has the baptism of Christ on one face. On the other faces the priest provides the seven sacraments: baptism, confirmation, communion (or mass), penance, extreme unction (the last rites), matrimony and ordination. At Salle, the font given by Thomas Line, his wife, and Robert, their son, has the crucifixion on the final side. For the eighth face of a seven-sacrament font the crucifixion and Christ's baptism are alternatives. Fonts of this type are found in twenty Norfolk village churches. The donor of the Salle font died in 1489; that at Walsoken dates to 1544. An interesting variant is the font at Blofield. The church dedicated to St Andrew and St

Peter is another large one. Both Sir Nikolaus Pevsner and Munro Cautley comment chiefly on the font. Rather than man, Christ himself is the inspiration for the stone carving: the nativity, the flight into Egypt, 'Ecce Homo', the mocking, the scourging, the crucifixion, the resurrection and the ascension.

Seven sacraments or none, the fonts of Norfolk village churches are fine whatever their date. Woodwork too exists in profusion; rarely is it not of high quality. Such was the wealth men lavished on their faith. It is part and parcel of a more grand design, the virtual wholesale rebuilding of churches from the wealth of wool in the fifteenth century. It is difficult to decide whether Mattishall or Salle is the earlier, or for that matter Cawston. They are broadly contemporary: Salle has the arms of King Henry V (1413–22) and a window extant in 1731 had an inscription referring to Thomas Boleyn (died 1411); St Agnes's, Cawston, owes its splendour to Michael de la Pole, Earl of Suffolk, who died in 1414; while architecturally All Saints', Mattishall, is of this time.

The wool broggers, the brokers between sheep farmers and weavers, met at Mattishall, south and west of most of the wool villages but despite its isolated position on the River Tud convenient for the exchange of fleeces. The grazing of sheep was done in the country round Swaffham, east of Lynn and west of Dereham. East Dereham itself is as far west as the wool villages go. Despite its market rights, East Dereham was little more than a large village in the fifteenth century. By then perhaps the church at Mattishall was largely complete. It is dated by the arcades separating nave from aisles: polygonal projections without capitals facing inwards and outwards while the arches have semicircular posts with capitals. A long way away is the church of St Mary the Virgin, Luton, Bedfordshire, but here again are polygonal projections, with polygonal posts this time and it is a good bet that these date from long before 1400: just before 1336 is a good guess. There seems no sound reason why the church at Mattishall should not be contemporary with the remains of its rood screen to which a fourteenth-century date has been applied. Before the Reformation the ceiling of the easternmost three bays of the hammer-beam roof was for the rood loft.

Of the rood screen at Mattishall only the lower part, the dado, remains. A much more complete screen is that at Cawston, for which a date about 1510 seems likely. But the screen is not the glory of Cawston, nor is the pulpit; it is the roof. There are few finer sights in the world than a Norfolk hammer-beam roof and at Cawston they did the world proud. There are angels on the wall braces, angels on the hammer-beams and they spread their wings in glorious array, neatly complementing the traceried spandrels of the parallelogram between beams, the verticals and the rafters. There is a sense of light at Cawston church, the interior contrasting with the hard exterior, but that is no less impressive. A tower of elephant-grey stone with its original medieval bell-frame intact, now holding pieces dated to 1658 and later, looks out on the town.

All men around 1500 had one overriding concern. Wool paid for their churches, but grain fed their bellies and brewed their only safe beverage. The plough was important, more so even than the spinning wheel. At Cawston there was a plough guild which had a guild hall, later the Plough Inn, whose sign came to lodge after 1950 in the parish church. The church had a plough gallery within the tower. The beam carries an inscription:

> God spede the plow
> And send us all corne enow
> Our purpose for to mak
> At crow of cok of ye plowlete of Sygate
> Be mery and glade
> Wat Goodale yis work mad.

Life was not all solemn: Wat Goodale was a church warden when the beam was raised and his name provided a pun on good cheer. The twentieth century has become used to a greater divorce between religion and life—a sad relic of the Victorian age—but in the Middle Ages the church was integral to village life. In addition to the plough guild Cawston had a guild dedicated to the Virgin, using the south transept as its chapel, and another dedicated to St Agnes, the patron saint of the church and in whose honour an annual fair was held on 21st January between 1300 and about 1550.

By 1550 the Middle Ages were over, wool was in retreat if not already in decline; thirty strangers and their families from the Netherlands received letters patent to settle in Norwich on 5th November 1565. The makers of Flemish stuffs, the New Draperies, had increased in numbers to 2,826 in 1569 and, despite the reputed deaths of 2,482 strangers in the plague of 1578–9, their number was recorded as 4,679 in 1582. The newcomers made Dutch bays, a heavier cloth than English worsted, and the new cloth became more popular than the old.

Religious practice too was different in the 1560s and 1570s from what it had been in the 1470s or the 1370s. In the late fourteenth century, men still made provision very much as their great-grandfathers had done in the 1270s, it was only the architectural style which developed. But occasionally a church was built all of a piece: Mattishall was one such. Another is the church of St Peter and St Paul, Salle. The first quarter of the fifteenth century is its date, with the transepts added certainly by the 1440s. Thomas Bigg paid for the south transept, the chapel of the Guild of St James (itself founded in 1358), and was buried there in 1444; the northern one has a brass of 1441. Salle church is not just big, it is huge. Walking away from Cawston to view this monument to man's belief in his own destiny the horizon is littered with tall towers: Cawston itself behind one to the east, Booton to the south (even if it is late Victorian) and the twin churches of Reepham and Whitwell to the west; while to the north are Heydon and Wood Dalling, with Guestwick just visible, and prominent to the fore is Salle itself. From a bus it is Salle not Cawston which one sees standing out across the valley from Brandiston and Haveringland, and it is Salle which one sees looking north from the Norwich to Fakenham road. Sheltered a little by a wood and by the trees of the churchyard the tower of Salle church, blunt and to the point about its intentions, stands sentinel and isolated. There are houses in Salle Street and the village school too, but this is a sparsely populated land: in the late twentieth century the people have fled into Aylsham and Cawston and Reepham, if not into Norwich. Perhaps it always was more attuned to sheep than to men, though corn is grown on these undulating slopes.

Church and water tower stand out for miles, but Salle is one of those churches which proclaims exactly what it is: a place imposed by men who wished their souls to be remembered. Thomas Bigg was one, Geoffrey Boleyn another, while the third was John Fountaine. A descendant of his, another John Fountaine, practised law in London, but when he died in 1671 they brought his body back to Salle to be buried on 25th June, eleven days after his death.

Coming on to Salle from Cawston, the interior is a shock. Cawston is light, Salle is darker but not dark. Cawston has arguably the finest of the Norfolk hammer-beam roofs, Salle in contrast seems plain. The painted ceiling is a very long way up, the bracing plain, almost uninteresting. It conveys none of the intimacy of the painted ceiling of Tivetshall St Margaret which extends by three boards above the nave walls: there are no aisles in this South Norfolk church. It is with inspection that the true importance of the roof of Salle church dawns on one. Building physics is a modern science concerned with stress and strain. A medieval carpenter, on the other hand, worked empirically. At Salle the nave roof is 8·54 metres (28 feet) wide, and a very long way up. Convention in the fifteenth century demanded a hammer-beam roof, but what the craftsmen built was ambitious and it worked. The nave roof starts (or finishes) in the aisle walls because these take the thrust. The principals of the aisle roofs go through the arcades and so form the corbels of the wall-posts of the nave roof. These wall-posts are long, dividing the clerestory into segments, each with a window, and above they become braces stretching up almost as far as the first purlins joining the rafters together. Salle roof has two lines of purlins, a very open construction on which someone took a gamble in 1430 or thereabouts. It worked but it could so easily have failed. Munro Cautley thirty years ago commented on the enormous strain on timber and walls made from the similar construction of the chancel roof at Salle. This had no aisles to help take the strain and only the smallest of braces in its 7·874 metres (25 feet 10 inches) width.

Priorities matter. It is the carpenter's courage, not the benefactor's bounty, which one remembers from Salle. With this church the village has come a long way from provision for itself and no greater size than the number of people who needed to stand or sit through a service. At Salle six guilds had altars and each needed space; that accounts a lot for the size. Surplus money and the lack of other suitable outlets for benefaction provide further reasons for the scale. No church of the scale of Salle can produce affection except with the long acquaintance which comes from regular worship there. Salle is not just a barn, open and devoid of the intimacy of long centuries of worship. Someone in the fifteenth century gave the church a wine-glass pulpit, so called from the narrow stem and the shape of the stand. At the beginning of the seventeenth century it was adapted into a Jacobean triple-decker with reading desk and clerk's seat below and sounding board above. Thomas, Lord Knyvett, gave the new pieces in 1611 but they seem to belong herein. About the font cover and its crane, one is not quite so sure. It is there when you walk in, but it is best viewed from the full length of the church. The crane makes it unusual: there is a pulley wheel above the contemporary brick font at Potter Heigham and the setting for a wheel above the later cover at Knapton; but the font cover at Salle is not the best in a Norfolk village church. That at Elsing is a century earlier and with the figures restored to the former glory of the medieval benefaction. Elsing church is all of a piece paid for by Sir Hugh Hastings who died in 1347. He is commemorated by an extravagant brass before the altar. Those who provide can expect for themselves the best seats in the synagogue.

There are other fifteenth-century font covers in Norfolk villages: Worstead and Castle Acre are two, Brancaster and South Acre two others. All like that at Salle have pinnacles to their peaks like church spires. Yet the one that is most striking, because it is so unexpected, is the disfigured piece in the corner of the north aisle of St Mary's Church, Kenninghall. Here the top does not imitate a church spire, it reflects instead an upturned wine glass. They went on making covers to fonts a long time after the Reformation. The one in Terrington St Clement is almost contemporary with King Henry's great matter in 1533 when he divorced Queen Catherine; the cover has paintings inside the casket which depict the baptism and the temptation of Our Lord, giving it the feel of some great triptych reminiscent of an altar piece. There are more in the seventeenth century: Walpole St Peter and Watlington, like the dated one of 1625 from Wiggenhall St Mary the Virgin, are from West Norfolk. They are found all over the county. Small and serviceable, and no less pleasing, is the small one at Stockton. Later still is that of 1704 at Knapton. Most visit the church of St Peter and St Paul in this remote village for the double-hammer-beam roof. Exactly two hundred years earlier than the font cover, with its multitude of angels. There are 138 in all that stare down from the span of 9·3 metres (30 feet 6 inches) across the nave; they did not bother with aisles.

Their font is thirteenth century; on it stands the attractive cover. No less attractive is the open but strangely large cover given to Long Stratton church a little over a century before the one at Knapton. Long Stratton has another survival from before the Reformation, a sexton's wheel, used to determine the days of the Lady Fast, kept for seven years as a penance.

At Salle there is too the original set of doors, one beneath the great west tower, one each in the north and south porches. Generously carved, they are most striking. The individual pieces at Salle church are good; it is the whole which is not quite satisfactory. There are doors again to other churches in other Norfolk villages which deserve to be remembered. The south door of Brooke church and that within the arched entry to the south of Great Snoring church belong equally to the fifteenth century. Even more magnificent is the south door of Martham church. Perhaps each of these three—Brooke, Great Snoring and Martham—succeed far more as impressing themselves as true village churches because that is what they are. There are bits of all ages within them. The roof of Great Snoring church, wide but not too wide, light, single framing and without elaboration above a tie beam comes, like its neighbour at St Andrew's, Little Snoring, as a relief from the masterworks of medieval carpentry displayed in hammer-beams and their great artistry. Necton church, away to the south, has soaring angels; in Ringland church the hammer-beams are hidden within the vaulting beside the clerestory. Even the cambered tie-beam roofs of the Norfolk–Suffolk–Cambridgeshire border area lack the simplicity of the roof of Great Snoring church. The group of tie-beam roofs is not large: Emneth, Methwold and with alternate arch braces and tie-beams Hockwold, are the Norfolk churches; Mildenhall and Lakenheath are in Suffolk, Isleham in Cambridgeshire. Their carpenter was a man of courage and ability. Did they breed them like that in great empty areas more fit for sheep than for men?

Methwold, Northwold and Feltwell are all compact villages within the sea of fen and common claimed from the earth. Hockwold is smaller but again the main centre of habitation is compact; it is joined to Wilton and the civil parish is one. The fen land is flat; the wool country undulating. But there are similarities of feeling between the two. The area of sheep and the area of wool are both empty—the stranger can wander at large and meet no one and see nothing except the distant landmark of a church tower.

Where, one might ask, in this profusion of fine churches are the villages? Where indeed, for the villages of this area of Norfolk are singularly non-existent. This undoubtedly has been the case for a long time. At their early Victorian height the population of parishes like Salle, Heydon and Thurning reached only 267, 321 and 166 respectively in 1841. At the same time 200 lived in Guestwick, 241 in Booton, while Brandiston, Haveringland and Little Witchingham numbered only 137, 160 and 45 persons respectively. Today the sparseness is more striking. Salle has only 79 people living there according to the 1971 census, a considerable decline on the 137 recorded ten years before. The electors list, affixed to the church door as is the case in Norfolk villages, is here a single typed sheet. It is not alone in housing under one hundred people: Thurning, Brandiston, Haveringland and Little Witchingham from those quoted are among the thirty-eight Norfolk villages with so miniscule a population.

When they are larger the people are spread out. Wood Dalling is a good example. In 1841, 560 people lived there, but this number had declined to 273 in 1961 and is today below the 185 recorded in 1971. The church is in the middle of the geographical parish. With a few exceptions the houses are in clusters north of it, at Foundry Hill, at Norton Corner, at Crabgate, at Red Pits, while Forest Farm, Tyby and Odessa are isolated as too is Wood Dalling Hall. Much of this is a new landscape, not of the time when St Andrew's Church was built.

It is not easy to reconstruct the scene wherein the famous Paston letters were written. Of the house at Paston where the family lived only the great barn remains. Built of flint, its length assumes primacy over all others in the county. It is 49·715 metres (163 feet) long. A similar barn at Waxham is shorter by a good ten metres. It is part of a complex built by the Wodehouse family during the fifteenth century. Only the encircling wall and gatehouse are as early; another gatehouse is Elizabethan, dating to the years of Thomas Wodehouse who after his death in 1571 was buried in Waxham church.

Between the surviving late medieval barns of Paston and Waxham is a bleak coast. The churches are gaunt against the sky: Palling, Lessingham (where the road goes inland), Happisburgh,

Walcott, Bacton and Paston itself. Behind the coast again the towers are high; Knapton takes the traveller inland again and on to Trunch. An old rhyme says:

> Gimingham, Trimingham, Knapton, Trunch,
> Northrepps, Southrepps, lie all in a bunch.

Here tied together in an old Soke (administrative unit), older by far than the Norman Conquest, lies a group of villages. The sea, except at Trimingham, is a parish away, but the wind blows hard. Even on a summer's day, the prevailing wind is from the north. The coast is wild and windswept. Happisburgh churchyard records more than one shipwreck and its victims. At Happisburgh they built a lighthouse in 1791, banded red and white; its beacon shines out relentlessly warning of the dangerous sands. The lighthouse is best appreciated from afar: the road from Sea Palling to Ingham is a good place to look north but the view is even more stunning from the road that runs between Winterton and Somerton or east from where the houses end at Martham. The view is of two church towers, Walcott and Happisburgh, and the lighthouse. From the south more towers can be seen and the high prominence of Winterton church speaks equally of the danger of the sea. The towers are big and strong, reassuring. Before the lighthouse was built, all sailors had was Walcott church and Happisburgh, too, with Horsey and Winterton to the south. The church towers stood out to guide ships beyond the sands. The sands have encroached now upon the land as the sea has driven relentlessly inwards. Eccles church, north-east of Lessingham, is two heaps of flint upon the sand. A gale sank its teeth into the tower in January 1895, but already the village was of "ruinated estate" in 1605. The sea has devoured Keswick too, as a local wise woman known as old Mother Shipton foretold: "Bacton Abbey shall be a farm and Keswick church a barn". Broomholm Priory is indeed a farmyard, piled high with rolled hay in the chapter house and across the cloister garth.

For six weeks, perhaps eight, the coast is more alive. Holidaymakers populate Bacton, Walcott and Sea Palling in late July and August but, come mid-September and through into May, the wilderness reigns. A single couple may shelter under the lie of the great stone boxes on Winterton beach but they have the sands to themselves. On a grey, blustery day in September, a courting couple can walk along the shoreline, oblivious of civilization and as far from it as the solitary swimmer on Sagres beach in April. The north-east corner of Norfolk and its villages is the end of England. To the north there is nothing but the sea, to the north-east it is a long way to Norway. The ravage is rarely far away. This is the land beyond the wool country proper, but churches along the coast and the barns too are contemporary with the splendour that the wealth of wool could erect.

And so to Trunch; from earlier reading the expectations are high. Bleak, windswept, lonely Trunch, yet it has all the makings of a most attractive village: stone is absent and flint is used, often to good effect. Farmhouses and cottages date to all periods from the fifteenth century onwards and to none. The village seems thriving, with shop and public house in the centre—but the public house is a shock. No pretty thing this, no attractive village inn, just a box of harsh yellow brick, unmellowed in its years, as much an intrusion now as the day it was built.

The church too seems unremarkable; that at least is the external impression of St Botolph's, Trunch. True the chancel door for the priest is enclosed in a porch and the south buttress of the chancel built on top of it. Only Beccles and Warham St Mary are akin in that respect. From the outside, however, the visitor might be inclined to give the church no second glance and go on his way to Knapton or Mundesley, to Gimingham or Southrepps. However, perhaps the clerestory suggests something more than the ordinary. It is the interior which commends Trunch. On the clerestory is hung an arch-braced, hammer-beam roof with the spandrels traceried like individually cut pieces of fretwork. Between nave and chancel is a screen, nothing unusual one might think, but this screen is more open than most and the paintings of the twelve apostles, if not well preserved, are at least discernible. The date is 1502. A pulpit of 1864 is in front of this; until then a very early sixteenth-century pulpit survived and possibly pews also. Certainly behind the screen are misericords of the fifteenth century.

All this would not take Trunch out of the ordinary. It is one of the churches to which Munro Cautley in *Norfolk Churches* gave four stars—not quite the highest category, for Salle and Walpole among the villages and St Peter Mancroft in Norwich gained five. But seven other churches were thought as significant: Terrington St Clement and West Walton on the marshlands of West Norfolk have no connection with wool and its profits, nor does the former abbey at Wymondham (over-rated this, its barrenness akin to the void and the emptiness of Seville Cathedral). Cley was the westernmost place where weavers are known to have worked; Ludham and Ranworth are on the south-east fringe of the wool zone; Cawston like Salle is central to the area and Trunch is on its north-east fringe. For that matter, St Peter Mancroft is partly a wool church too; it is, I know, many other things too, not least from its date (begun 1430 and consecrated in 1455) one of the finest examples of early Renaissance building in England, fit to be compared with the only slightly later King's College Chapel at Cambridge.

For St Peter Mancroft, one expects things of the highest order; for Trunch, quite frankly, one does not have the same anticipation. At St Peter Mancroft the font canopy is hidden away in a corner—one could miss it at the first visit—but at Trunch one only has to open the door of St Botolph's Church. It is there, glorious, bold, light, airy, affirmative. Outside Norfolk there are only two other font canopies in England. A nasty monstrosity of 1300 or thereabouts affronts each newly wed couple in the parish church of St Mary the Virgin, Luton, Bedfordshire. The Bishop of Durham, John Cosin, in 1662 gave one to his cathedral. Atop the Norwich one is a pelican above the octagonal superstructure built up on four columns. At Trunch the craftsman raised six columns around 1500. Richly carved with grapes and vines, it is excellent workmanship. On the superstructure above, the paintings are not all extant: Christopher Dowsing in 1643 saw to that, if not some earlier despoiler. One or other removed the flying buttresses which connected the top to the base. In 1552, copes, vestments, altar-cloths and bells became forfeit to the greedy men who served Edward VI. They were scarcely less rapacious than the men who less than a generation earlier had served his father.

The inexplicable zeal for destruction seems always to accompany an operation designed to cleanse a body of its iniquities. It was they who tore down the rood lofts of Norfolk churches; little did they think of how much care and craftsmanship men had lavished on the faith they had loved; little did they remember that their fathers' fathers, if not in that village then in another, had given money for the building of the structure between nave and chancel.

The splendour of wool was over for Norfolk villages by the time Sir Christopher Heydon, Sir John Robsart and Sir William Fermore came to the church of St Botolph at Trunch. For some reason these men, of Baconsthorpe, of Stanfield Hall and of East Barsham Manor, left alone the great font canopy. They did not raze it; we do not know who gave the structure about fifty years before their visit; perhaps he was then known. A similar saving happened in villages a century later: least mutilated were the monuments to the generation which had just died.

For its size, Norfolk has comparatively few monuments of the generation before the English Civil War; their discussion belongs to the chapter which follows. Of brasses, too, the earlier fashion, the villages of Norfolk have little of prominence. At Worstead, there remain indents (impressions in the stone where metal has been) but except in two cases, one of which is to John Arblaster, there is no latten plate. At Salle the profusion is greater, especially from the 1440s. Geoffrey Boleyn died in 1441, Thomas Roose in 1441, John Funteyn (Fountaine) in 1453 and John Brigge in 1454; each has a brass and another for his wife or three in the case of John Funteyn. The mortality of man is represented by John Brigge's brass: a skeleton in a shroud.

Perhaps it was this mortality which made men lavish not upon their church but upon themselves in another part of Norfolk. In the villages south of the River Yare and east of the River Tas, the buildings may be contemporary but they are rarely ecclesiastical. The exception is the church of St Martin at New Buckenham. A man buried in the building, John Coke, left money for its building in 1479, a century later than Worstead was begun.

There is a contrast here between Norfolk villages. If wool villages lavished money on their churches, the prosperity was not less in the arable lands south-west of Norwich but the splendour went into the timber-framed buildings of the old market square at New Buckenham, isolated farmhouses at Tacolneston and the Forncetts, and the rare minor manor house. There is another area of late medieval farming prosperity north and west of this: the Rocklands, St Peter and All Saints, are poor examples, Caston little better, but Great Ellingham reflects something of the grain harvests which were good in the reigns of Edward IV, Henry VII and Henry VIII. These are grainlands today and have been throughout the past five hundred years. A decayed windmill at Northacre, where Caston ends and Griston begins, retains bits of the sails, but one at Great Ellingham was burnt out in a fire.

Great Ellingham retains a number of late medieval timber-framed houses, each with a thatched roof. None is spectacular, but they have stood for a good half millennium and that makes them more than mediocre. Only that which is well built and properly conceived will stand the ravages of weather for so long a time span. Another good house is Church Farmhouse, Caston, where a brick gable is decorated with vertical panelling. Flint is more usual here than timber, but Old Hall, Great Ellingham, is timber-framed to the core. Remodelled with later sixteenth-century wings, it began life no doubt as an open hall about a hundred years earlier.

Elizabeth I came to the throne in 1558; a century earlier, 1450 say, was only a hundred years after the Black Death. It used to be thought that the economy of England was so depressed for such a long time afterwards that it was not until the early sixteenth century that rejuvenation began. Wool churches in East Anglia are proof against this simplistic hypothesis at its most extreme. But viewed systematically, the weight of benefaction: fonts, screens, even roofs—all the splendid array of late medieval craftsmanship—is predominantly to be dated after the Battle of Tewkesbury (1471) and mostly to beyond the Battle of Bosworth (1485). Nevertheless, most of it was in place and in use by the time Henry VIII became king in 1509. Much of the weight of survival is because this was the last, and most prosperous, generation of benefaction and earlier gifts have been lost. On the other hand this is the first generation from which timber-framed buildings survive in any quantity.

New Buckenham has a considerable number of timber-framed buildings. Not all are as old as the fifteenth century: the market house on the village green dates to the seventeenth century. That building may show the latest use of timber at New Buckenham; brick took over as the building material thereafter. The village smithy almost opposite the market house, where the road from Norwich cuts a swathe through the square, may be almost as old as its neighbour. A great number of the buildings in New Buckenham are much older. Many have an overhang to the first floor.

There are buildings with a jetty long-side on to the street and at least one whose gable-end is jettied. On the road south from the green where it turns sharply west is a large house, now a single dwelling, but in its time both a series of cottages (for more than one blocked door can be seen) and earlier a farmhouse with an attached barn. On the north side of the green is a different house, now three cottages each occupying a bay. On the two outside bays the first floor is jettied, the centre is set back flush with the line of the ground-floor wall. The tradition behind this is foreign to Norfolk. Originating in Kent and Sussex, the "Wealden House" is known elsewhere in Norfolk villages. There is one covered with clapboarding on the green at West Acre and another with its medieval screens, or entrance, passage surviving at Fir Tree Farm, Forncett St Mary, originally the manor house of Williams Manor. Perhaps others survive, altered now, with the jetty made continuous, or even with an eighteenth-century or later brick front hiding the timber work completely.

New Buckenham has a regular plan. This is deliberate. It is the earliest piece of town planning in England. William d'Albini moved his castle to a corner of the parish of Old Buckenham in 1145. He built there the earliest circular keep in the country; part still survives despite the demolitions of Sir Philip Knyvett in the 1640s. There is an earlier castle in Old Buckenham, but of this and its successor, the Augustinian priory, nothing remains. East of his new castle, William d'Albini laid out a town in a chequerboard pattern, four streets running north-south, four running east-west. As a town it did not prosper, in contrast to Attleborough to the north, and today its inhabitants refer to it as a village.

A village too is Pulham Market, marginally less in hectares than its neighbour, Pulham St Mary. The latter has 1,226 hectares for its farmlands, Pulham Market makes do with 1,208 hectares (respectively 3,030 acres and 2,984 acres), but half as many people again live in Pulham Market. In 1971, the respective populations were 905 for the larger place, 657 for the smaller. New Buckenham is smaller, with only 297 people.

Around the village green of Pulham St Mary Magdalen, the true name of Pulham Market, the late medieval farmers built their houses; superb thatched houses, not puny cottages. There are three to the east and one to the north, behind a later public house, The Falcon. Facing the green to the south is another of the village hostelries, The Crown. Thatched and timber-framed, with inside doorways and windows preserved from the early fifteenth-century building (if not a generation before that), this shows the cycle of farmhouse to cottages and back to a single dwelling, albeit as a public house. There are four chimney-stacks surviving and one has been removed. The last, now shown by a patch of new thatch on the ridge, and those at either end may be later than the sixteenth century, but the great double chimney occupying the former screens passage is part of the continuing farming prosperity of the Tudor years. That prosperity began earlier; it can be seen in The Crown at Pulham Market. The end bay, marked off by a row of studs, denoting a former wall, was the solar, the private quarters for the owner and his wife. Here the best woodwork is in the arched doorway, the diamond-sectioned verticals to the windows, and the studding which if not close-set is less widely spaced than elsewhere in the building. The former hall portion does duty as the lounge of the public house; the area west of the chimney was the kitchen area, now it is the public bar. It is a nice, if unconscious, survival of the arrangements of a late medieval house.

The late medieval village in Norfolk, as elsewhere in England, had two basic plans. One was the farmhouses round the village green; the other placed some of the farmhouses out in the centre of the fields they served. The two Pulhams were not enclosed until 1838; the plan of Pulham Market reflects this; it is an example of the first type of village cited. Forncett St Mary reflects the other type. Here the farmhouses, as at Tacolneston to the west, are scattered on the roads nearer their fields. Some villages by their situation have neither plan. These are road villages like Long Stratton, spread out along the Norwich to Ipswich road, with some late medieval buildings surviving. There seemed less prosperity there than to the east or the west, although the church dedicated to St Mary has riches. These, however, are more generally of the seventeenth century than the fifteenth.

With the Tudors, the fifteenth century gave way to the sixteenth. Change was in the air, changes men did not like, changes men could not abide. England was peaceful in Henry VIII's years and those of his daughter Elizabeth, but his son's reign was a different picture. Edward VI was a mere boy manipulated by the more gross elements of his father's council who garnered to themselves the kingly functions. Men felt safer in challenging authority then: our next chapter will show the resplendent power the Tudor state sought to have in Elizabeth's day as it attempted to overawe the populace.

The people of Norfolk were not overawed by the mere gentry of the county nor even in his absence by the Duke of Norfolk. Neither were they afraid to express their grievances. In June, July and August 1549 there came to the county a violent thunder of indignation. Robert Kett, a prosperous yeoman of Wymondham, led the protesters. A landlord, not a tenant, he might more have sympathized with the enclosing of commons for sheep and for efficient farming. Himself obliged to tear down his own fences, he pursued a quarrel with a neighbour, Sir John Flowerdew. Religion too had its part to play in the Norfolk revolt. Much that was familiar was destroyed with the Reformation. Religious houses especially were victims of the changes. Wymondham Abbey became the target of a man's greed. That man was Sir John Flowerdew. He had stripped the lead from the roof of the church and he had carted away the bells from the tower, yet Wymondham Abbey was not his property; the townsmen of Wymondham had bought the church and the monastic buildings for continuing use as the parish church. Hitherto, the nave alone had served. The feast of the translation of Thomas Becket to Canterbury, 7th July, was traditionally a day of celebration in Wymondham. On that day, 1549, the commotion erupted.

Hedges on Flowerdew's land were thrown down. This had happened before, in fact as recently as 20th June at nearby Attleborough, but there are earlier instances of disturbances caused by the erection of fences and hedges to mark newly enclosed lands. Five years before, in 1544, at Great Dunham a mob with pitchforks had assembled to assert their rights to common pasture. At Hingham a protracted dispute was levied by the freeholders against Sir Henry Parker for his enclosure of the wastes of the village. He was threatened with violence and with the loss of his sheep. He had put six hundred on the commons, overstocking the pasture intended both for cattle and for sheep. Kett's Rebellion need never have been more than a local grievance, centred on Wymondham. It became a national scandal. It involved the whole county, although some parts less than others. Robert Kett and his band marched on Norwich, quartered themselves on Mousehold

Heath, still an open space, and defied the established order for six weeks. There the good ordering of the people, some six thousand in all, was in the hands of fifty men, elected as governors by their fellows from the hundred wherein they resided. Nine hundreds were not represented: the more limited nature of Robert Kett's support is clearly brought out. No governors were appointed for Freebridge Marshland, Clackclose and Grimshoe Hundreds on the county's south-western fringe, nor for Smithden and Docking Hundreds in the north-west corner, neither were they for a southern group of hundreds, Earsham, Diss, Guiltcross, Shropham and Wayland. Only Freebridge Lynn and South Greenhoe Hundreds are represented among the governors of those hundreds of Norfolk more than a day's journey from Norwich. Kett's followers came from the wool lands north and east of Norwich and from the grainlands to the south.

When Robert Kett drew up a series of twenty-nine demands, their content was economic, emphasizing the decaying splendour of wool. They reflect the continuing greed of men. Wool profits were long maturing not into fine churches but into the visitations of the King's heralds from the College of Arms. Robert Kett fulminated against men who had by purchase and by more subtle means made themselves masters of great tracts. The process, technically known as engrossing, was the first stage of building a landed estate. It was already underway and too far advanced by 1549 to see other than a new age in Norfolk villages: the Age of the Visitations.

A conservative, almost a reactionary, Robert Kett hardly represented the ordinary man; in distance, he was too far removed from the poor of the sixteenth century, the real sufferers of enclosure, engrossing and inflation. Governments ultimately triumph, especially ones as well organized as the Tudor state. In August 1549, the Earl of Warwick came to Norwich and offered pardon to all except the Wymondham yeoman. Kett was inclined to accept the offer but it was ultimately refused. By the end of the month, three thousand men had died, the victims of superior technology: staves and pitchforks were never a match for guns and disciplined cavalry. They found Robert Kett soon after the débâcle; condemned for treason, he swung from a gibbet at Norwich Castle on 7th December. His brother, William, another prosperous citizen of Wymondham, the authorities hung from the great west tower of Wymondham Abbey. On the road east of the town, halfway to Hethersett, there is a gnarled oak tree, Kett's Oak, where the leader addressed the people and urged them on to Norwich and to his own death. Four hundred years later in memory of misdeed a plaque was placed beside the entrance to Norwich Castle. It reads:

> In 1549 A.D. Robert Kett, yeoman farmer, of Wymondham was executed by hanging in this castle after the defeat of the Norfolk rebellion of which he was leader. In 1949 A.D. four hundred years later this memorial was placed here by the citizens of Norwich in reparation and honour to a notable and courageous leader in the long struggle of the common people of England to escape from a servile life into the freedom of just conditions.

With Kett's Rebellion the age of wool closed; the Reformation had destroyed much of the context of the late medieval church and the orgy of destruction had already begun so soon after men had given their surplus profits for rood screens, for font covers, for choir stalls, for angel roofs (although the last-named were spared). In the Age of the Visitations it was the secular which led.

IV

Villages and Visitations

SIXTEENTH-CENTURY England was a status-conscious age; its seventeenth-century successor even more so. Men aspired to the right to be called by the title of "gentleman". Landed wealth was the criterion which conferred the status for which men had striven. Of course, such things had to be done properly; it was not just a question of the aspirant adopting the title, he had to be vetted. An elaborate procedure was instituted about 1530 to enquire into the lineage of those who wished to claim one of the privileges of a gentleman: the right to bear a coat of arms. The College of Arms was established in 1483. By 1558, when Elizabeth I became Queen of England, their work had not proceeded very far. A few counties had been visited in 1530, but times were troubled thereafter for a generation. As with Norfolk, the first visitation of a county usually dates to the 1560s.

William Hervey, Clarencieux King of Arms, came to Norfolk in 1563. His successor, Robert Cooke, came in 1589, while in 1613 the Richmond Herald, John Raven, enquired of the county who was of the "port and carriage of a gentleman". The Civil War put a stop to the making of visitations, but after the Restoration Sir Edward Bysshe, knight, the Clarencieux King of Arms, came in 1664 to enquire again. The final investigation, a full generation since its predecessor, bears out the famous quotation of a Norfolk man. Sir Thomas Browne of Great Walsingham had no illusions when he penned the words: "Generations pass and old families last not three oaks."

He could have truthfully added, nor a single Spanish chestnut. In the churchyard of Hevingham, beside the church porch, a sapling was planted in 1610. The splendid tree had reached a girth of 12 feet 7 inches in 1742. Forty years later it was measured again. In 1782 the girth was 15 feet 0½ inch, four inches more than in 1778. When Arthur Young measured the tree, 4 feet 11½ inches above the ground on one side and 4 feet 4 inches upon the other, as had been done previously, he found it had increased again by ten and a half inches in the twenty years up to 1802. The girth was then 15 feet 11 inches. At its most recent measurement, in 1970, the girth was 19 feet. There are other Spanish chestnuts, none quite so fine, and old oaks too in the churchyard and rectory garden at Hevingham. The trees which line Morningthorpe Green look no less ancient than those of the Broadland churchyard beside the Norwich to Aylsham road. The South Norfolk row, a dozen in all, was planted and growing, certainly when the last of the visitations was made, if not that of 1613. Compared with such antiquity, man is indeed short-lived. His forbears, too, might be uncertain, like the Dawbney family of Sharrington who noted seven generations of males before a wife could be remembered and two more before her father's full name could be recorded in the pedigree noted in the visitations. Some men could not recall even that: John Lynghoke of Terrington, who was twice married, could give only his parents and maternal grandfather, his two wives and their fathers and his own five children. Elaborate pedigrees belonged only to the very richest and best-placed of men like the Hobarts of Hales; they are exceptional.

Yet for all the rarity of detail in noting medieval forbears, the visitations of Norfolk, amalgamated into a single collection about 1620, provide an introduction to their age. Elizabeth's reign and that of her two Stuart successors is the Age of the Visitations: status conscious, peopled by men who strove in their own small world to impose their will and thereby to stamp their mark.

Land for them was of paramount importance. Some rose from nothing to rate a funeral not in St Peter Mancroft, not in a country church, not in a London city church but in that epitome of success itself, St Paul's Cathedral, London. Sir Thomas Gresham was one, he who noted what governments heed not to their peril: that bad money drives out good and the result is inflation. Thomas Gresham had long Norfolk connections, in Gresham and in Holt. His brother-in-law was a lawyer, Sir Nicholas Bacon, to whom

Norfolk was neither ancestral nor central: he was a Suffolk man yet he bought land in Norfolk at Stiffkey, at Thraxton, at Brissingham, at Stody and at Eccles. He built elsewhere, in Suffolk at Redgrave Hall, and on Verulamium's empty waste at Gorhambury; he built, too, on a minor scale in Norfolk. A truncated Stiffkey Hall remains above the village, but much is ruined now and part visible only as stumps of walls. A gentry family veering towards bankruptcy for years, the Banyards sold the site to Bacon, a man with a considerable progeny who did not wish to impoverish his children. The builder was his second son, Nathaniel, who himself was married to a natural daughter of Sir Thomas Gresham. Most of the Bacon lands in Norfolk went to him and from Sir Thomas he received manors in Langham, Morston and Hemsby. He settled down on the rent roll to be a country gentleman of the age: sheriff of the county in 1599 and member of parliament in 1583, 1593 and 1604. He was among those knighted at the coronation of James I. *The Stiffkey Papers*, the collection of his correspondence edited in 1915 and 1936, show his life as a magistrate. Gentry were the backbone of Norfolk society and the leaders of Norfolk villages in the Age of the Visitations.

All that Nathaniel Bacon lacked to found a dynasty on the north Norfolk coast was sons. His daughters married well: a Townsend of Raynham, a Knyvett of Wymondham and a Gawdy of Claxton. To the eldest, Joanne (or Ann), he gave the heirloom of a silver cup, now at Raynham Hall. With Raynham Hall Tudor building in Norfolk ceases. The earliest parts date from 1622 but the house was successively remodelled after 1672 and again by William Kent for the celebrated "turnip Townsend" in the 1720s. The house was begun at just the moment when another Norfolk great house was going up at Blickling Hall, bought by Sir Henry Hobart in 1616, who between 1620 and 1627 used Robert Lyminge to build the house: Lyminge, who also built Hatfield House, is buried at Blickling and there recorded as "the architect and builder of Blickling Hall".

These are a far cry from each other but also from the earliest great houses of Norfolk villages. Among these must be included the old hall at Raynham. It is of brick and stands not far from the church. It is not the earliest, for that is the well-known Caister Castle built by Sir John Fastolf between 1432 and 1435 out of the profits of the French wars. The surviving parts of Sir Henry

Heydon's Baconsthorpe Castle are a full generation later but this building of the 1480s is of stone. Brick was used here only in the later, sixteenth century, parts but by then the new material of the 1430s had become established.

One of the earliest places in England where brick became the established building material for the great house dominating the village was West Norfolk. The original structure of Middleton Towers, built by Lord Scales before 1460 and by his son-in-law in the decade after, is reduced now to a gatehouse: the main house was rebuilt in 1860 and again in 1900. Snore Hall, Fordham, is contemporary with the famous Oxburgh Hall, for which licence to crenellate was given to Edward Bedingfeld in 1482. A later Bedingfeld, Sir Henry, in 1581 was assessed to have lands valued at £200, five times as much as anyone else in South Greenhoe Hundred and by the same margin over all the other sixteen people assessed on lands in Oxborough that year. The great house of the villages of Tudor Norfolk was built by a man whose distance from his fellows was marked by that much and by more in the cold statistics of tax gathering. A remarkable listing survives for nearly all of Norfolk for three generations earlier than 1581. Henry VIII needed to replenish his royal coffers in 1523. He besought each county to list the men and their wealth, particularly those of more than the average level of wealth. The minimum level of assessment in Sir Roger Townsend's listing was lands to the value of forty pounds, or goods to the same. The majority are at that but a few stand out, those with above one hundred pounds. Launditch, South Greenhoe, Wayland and Grimshoe Hundreds are missing but for the rest, the villages could raise only eighteen men. A merchant at Lynn and Bedingfeld make the total a score. For the richest there is a correlation with the earliest brick buildings.

Roger Townsend was not quite the richest man assessed in Norfolk; his lands were computed at £600. One had slightly more than he, Sir Henry Fermour, at a thousand marks (£666 13s 4d). East Barsham manor reflects a wealth built on wool; the flocks on twenty-five grounds numbered seventeen thousand and more. The Townsends, too, were rich in wool; a son's account for a portion of the flock total numbered four thousand in the late 1540s. On these profits the great houses were built. At Wiggenhall St Mary the gatehouse of St Mary's Hall in part at least belongs to the

Great Massingham and its pond

North Lopham

The village sign at Sea Palling

Thorpland Hall

The surviving portion of the tower of Rocklands St Andrew church

Saxon church at Framlingham Earl

(*Opposite*) The wool broggers' church at Mattishall

Restored windmill at Horsey Mere, built 1912

Plough outside Mattishall church

Barn at Claxton

The fields of Kenninghall

Haystack at Hales

Silos at Kirby Cane

Brooke mere

house built by the Kervile family around 1500. Humphrey Kervile was among the wealthy men of the county in 1523 but the family died out in 1624 and the house has subsequently been much altered, especially during the Victorian period. Chimneys and battlements, all restored, stand out across the fen. Fitton Hall is a little later, an early Tudor house of deep red brick, on the boundary of Wiggenhall St Germans and Wiggenhall St Peter. A curious sight and in plan cruciform, it retains the original mullioned windows.

An important group of buildings dates to around 1525. They include a number of houses at one time in their history used as the village rectory. At Upwell, the whole house is of brick, but at Methwold only a gable end is, the rest of the house is timber-framed. Contemporary are three: Great Snoring Rectory, Fincham Hall and the great mass of the manor house at East Barsham. Sir Henry Fermour built the house and the gatehouse in the 1520s: house first, because there the royal arms in stone have griffin and greyhound while those in brick on the gatehouse have griffin and lion and so date its construction to after 1527, the year in which the supporters of the royal arms were changed.

The road from Fakenham bends slightly before approaching the house, a coppice obscures the view. The road beyond rises sharply, after dipping to the vale of the River Stiffkey. In size it is a shock, for the house while restored in 1919 and made habitable in the ruined part in 1938 is less than when first built—a parallel block adjacent to the gatehouse has been demolished. It is less than a single pavilion of the eighteenth-century Holkham Hall, not that far to the north. One is at once struck by the house's splendour, for here is brickwork of the highest quality; no pastiche could ever be so magnificent, no film set could ever aspire to such excellence. The brickmaker's art is not easy to learn and here it is applied with dark force both in the set of royal arms and in the friezes and the pinnacles. The great block of carved and twisted chimneys at the centre of the house completes the picture.

One leaves East Barsham with the feeling that one would like to know more: the house is not open to the public, a notice proclaims, and an owner's privacy should be respected. East Barsham otherwise is one of the most disappointing villages of Norfolk. Only a village school, with its playground marked for hop-scotch and other games, relieves the monotony. The church here is over-restored, mutilated in the worst Victorian way, and like the bare floor of the village pub breathes a sense of the depressing which should be absent, for this is beautiful country, no less beautiful than the better-known and justly-celebrated Glaven valley to the east. Of all Norfolk's rivers, the River Stiffkey is the least well known.

At East Barsham the river follows a meandering course that goes first south-east, then east and then north before going east again and then south-east. Before the river bends north to Great Snoring there was once another village, Thorpland. Thorpland Hall occupies the site, another creation of the Fermours: Sir Henry Fermour was indicted in the Court of Star Chamber in 1520 for encroaching upon the land. The house is a range only now, of brick both red and white, with red brick buttresses and chimney-shafts, contemporary no doubt with East Barsham manor house. Viewed from above, Thorpland Hall is approached by an avenue of trees, one partly fallen across the grass drive; it looks and is a great house but at the same time the house is a home.

Great Snoring is north of Thorpland on a climbing road that dips to the river and rises again. At Great Snoring there is perhaps the most perfect village in Norfolk, a street of sensible houses of various styles leading down from the church to the river bridge and with the small village green at the opposite end to the church. The church, light and airy, stands adjacent to the factory, but that is a misnomer for this house. It only became the rectory after it had ceased to be the manor house. The Shelton family held sway here: a Sir Ralph Shelton, died 1424, is buried to the north of the altar of St Mary's Church. A descendant, also Sir Ralph Shelton, built the manor house beside the church. Shrouded in trees, and thus difficult to photograph, only a part remains of the original structure. That portion is altered with an eighteenth-century front, but one piece at an obtuse angle to the rest retains the sculptured front of moulded bricks carrying the frieze recording the initials of Christ and his Mother:

M IHS M IHS M

between the ground floor and the first floor. There is another, less elaborate, frieze of balusters and heads above the first floor which continues along a front now otherwise rendered with plaster. At the corners are polygonal turrets which rise above the level of the roof, suggesting once a design intended to incorporate another storey.

The great bulk of Oxburgh Hall is three storeys; the polygonal turrets have fine lines of corbel tables (decorative brickwork raised out from the face) within the same height and go on up beyond for two more friezes and the battlements. The great house has two fellows in West Norfolk, St Mary's Hall at Wiggenhall St Mary and, across the River Great Ouse, Watlington Hall. Far to the east is the site of another of these great palaces, Shelton Hall. Gone now, it had all the magnificence of the great house: courtyard and hall, ranges and curtain walls. The future Queen Elizabeth spent much of her childhood here with her great aunt, Lady Shelton, and her uncle, Sir John Shelton. Here she had her own pew, now vanished, in the village church. Shelton church is totally of brick, except for vaulting in the porch, a piece of the tower, and corbels in the nave and quoins and buttresses. It lacks a chancel. Perhaps the son was less assiduous than his father, Sir Ralph Shelton (died 1487). As with St Peter Mancroft in Norwich there is an eastern sacristry; it might have been all that was originally intended. Inside Shelton church there is now only the dado of the rood screen dividing nave and aisles off from the priest's end, but once this would at its full height have marked a chancel, and churches enough in Norfolk villages have nave and chancel in one. St Mary's, Hemsby, and St Mary's, Burgh St Peter, are two, both older by a century in the case of the first-named and by two in that of the latter than Sir Ralph Shelton's building in his eponymous village. The church certainly looks complete. Yet it is not; the south porch lacks the upper parts of the vaulting to the ground floor and the visitor stares up into the void of an upper chamber with unplastered brick. The interior, however, is laid bare with plaster, and a plain flat roof. Very bare it is too, and here the unfinished feeling is most strong, for clearly the corbels were meant to take a more ambitious roof, and at the east end the tombs of the Sheltons are to the south plain and to the north with an incomplete canopy. The church has one Jacobean monument, to Sir Robert Houghton (died 1623), and that rearranged on the south side of the chancel aisle. The Shelton family had by then ceased to be landowners in the parish; another had taken their place within a hundred years of when they had numbered among the twenty richest families of the county.

Churches in South Norfolk have nowhere quite the total use of brick seen at Shelton, but there are pieces no less delightful for that. Away above the marshes in the great bend of the River Waveney are Wheatacre and Burgh St Peter. At Wheatacre church, brick is combined with flint for a chequer-board effect on the walls of the tower, but the jambs of a doorway (now blocked) and the window above use the new material. At Burgh St Peter, the church of St Mary has a most curious tower, designed as a set of individual boxes arranged in five steps. It imitates an Italian creation that a vicar's son saw in 1790, but the two lowest stages are Tudor brick and flint with a diaper. At Claxton church the south porch is brick with polygonal corner towers. Much of the church tower is brick too.

There are the remains of a castle in Claxton, now represented by a single long wall with three semicircular towers, two flanking a blocked entrance arch. The walls are basically of flint but with much brick inserted and there is considerable evidence of brick having been used for the jambs to the entrance. Henry Gawdy died here in 1620, and a monument was erected by his son in 1637 in Claxton Church, but the castle predates the ownership of the village by the family. It was probably their home and demolished early in the eighteenth century. The present manor house looks to be Victorian but has earlier portions, and a long barn in the adjacent farmyard has a date of 1706. Almost opposite is a contemporary barn, seemingly not connected with the manor house.

There are houses in South Norfolk surviving from the early Tudor years. Hales Hall is only a single range and a barn of a much greater house. Built on a courtyard plan by Sir James Hobart, attorney general to Henry VII, it lay west of the remaining structures, a long gatehouse range facing a barn of equal antiquity: both are roofed as they were originally, thatched barn and tiled domestic range. The gateway, a simple opening flanked by narrow piers, opens to the great green which once stood between Hales Hall and Loddon Hall. It also gave a way for the Hobarts to drive to Loddon church: it was their creation, Sir James rebuilt it in the late fifteenth century and his descendants were buried there in 1541, 1561 and 1613.

East of Loddon and north of the River Chet is Hardley Hall, another large sixteenth-century house, of brick and flint with stone dressings and a diaper pattern of diamond-shaped lozenges on the west end. Most of the fenestration was redone in the eighteenth century and later but the house retains an original door and doorway which may suggest that the present building remodels an earlier house. As a single range, one room deep, its plan reflects arrangements much earlier than the date of around 1530 which has been suggested both for the stonework of the window surrounds and for the four fireplaces which have been uncovered. One of the latter was on the first floor, showing that the house was from the Tudor period two-storeyed.

There are many manor houses from Elizabethan and slightly later times in Norfolk villages. They are spread out on many of the roads radiating from Norwich. Gowthorpe Manor, east of Swardeston, is a house with two dates, 1574 on the porch and 1669 on a gable, but the latter is probably a retouching. At Mulbarton there is the Old Hall with its Dutch gable, repeated on the barn, a seventeenth-century building rather than an earlier one. Mergate Hall, at Bracon Ash, is a house which looks late Georgian and indeed has dates of 1789 and 1790 on outbuildings but it is much altered and a more probable date for the original building would seem to be the 1580s or the early 1600s: the harvests were atrocious in the 1590s and little building was undertaken. Somewhat earlier than this is Dairy Farmhouse, Tacolneston, a remarkable house with the end walls of brick and the long walls timber-framed. The brick gables, stepped and with great solid chimneys, look original; the range has pargetting on the front which is broken by a triple-gabled porch and there is a rear staircase of three storeys, each smaller than the one below. This may have been once a minor manor house. It was not the principal manor house of the village. There are other, larger houses in Tacolneston which may be that. The Old Hall is probably late seventeenth-century but with an earlier core. The Queen Anne house known as Tackleston Hall is very handsome indeed and one of the most ordered houses in the county.

No one could call Long Stratton composed: untidy and strung out would be more apposite. Yet in this place lining the Norwich to Ipswich road, a very humble house indeed, timber-framed, low and now ill-cared for, has a brick gable with dumpy chimneys as its southern wall. Brick had ceased to be the preserve of the mighty and the church. Yet ordinary mortals still built largely in timber and daub. At Long Stratton, there is some indication of the prosperity of Tudor farming, for the village was rebuilt in the sixteenth century.

Another village largely rebuilt at this time is Kenninghall, a single street on the way which leads out to Kenninghall Place. These were the houses of village craftsmen and their contemporaries who tilled the soil, the husbandmen.

The houses of Kenninghall are individually far removed in wealth, prestige and style from what is probably the last Elizabethan house in a Norfolk village, Kirkstead Hall of 1614, a full decade after the glorious queen's death. The chimney-shafts reflect traditions of her father's reign. Only the plan with a central entrance conforms to the date. This is distinctly a house designed for the gentry but it is of sensible size and eminently intended to be lived in. It has a mark of authority but that extends no more than the bounds of the parish.

The houses of the gentry and of lesser men were built on the profits of the Tudor price rise. Norfolk villagers from 1520 lived through an inflation their forefathers had not known; nor were their descendants in the eighteenth century and the Victorian age to experience the same. Only the twentieth century has seen the same momentum in the rise in the cost of living. On the profits of the good years the rebuilding was done. Yeoman farmers invested their profits in solid farmhouses and in improvements to existing dwellings with the division of large houses into less open structures. Privacy, not the exclusive privacy of the twentieth century, but nevertheless a need for less communal living, became a requirement. Fireplaces were inserted into the big medieval farmhouses of Tacolneston and Forncett St Peter and the somewhat smaller ones at Great Ellingham; the houses lining the village green at Pulham Market were improved too, and one may have been built about 1580.

Elsewhere big new farmhouses were also built. An early example, of her father's rather than Elizabeth's reign is the clapboarded and timber-framed house north of the green at West Acre of which a photograph is included in the plates. Its wealth stands out, even in its present shuttered and nailed-up state. West Acre is a pleasant little spot, the kind of place at which a travelling topographer does not mind being marooned for an hour between buses in the middle of the day. The prevailing building material is flint; brick is used for the more recent cottages. The farmhouse was two cottages when last occupied, and it had been so tenanted for a hundred years and more before. When it was built this was the home of a prosperous yeoman, a man who felt confident of his achievements and could place himself solidly in a new house on the village green. Among timber-framed buildings in Norfolk it stands out. The façade is divided into three units, irregularly spaced but with a single roof which is hipped at both ends. The two outer units have overhanging first floors, but the jetty is not present in the centre; in this house the western side is also jettied. This usual 'Kentish' feature in a house unusual in its form for Norfolk emphasizes both that this was once an isolated building without the range of houses on its north side and that the builder was full of confidence. It was perhaps too ambitious, for at some point in time the west jetty has had to be underpinned. The posts are in front of the packing on which the original sill beam was placed. Within the stones are lumps of squared masonry; the stones of West Acre Priory doubtless provided a convenient quarry in the 1540s.

There are other villages, too, with houses as prosperous and as ambitious as that on the green at West Acre. Manor Farm, Pulham Market, is one such where the screen separating entrance from principal room, still called the hall, survives in a timber-framed house of the sixteenth century. There is a jettied farmhouse on the road south of Shipdham which looks again like the prosperous yeoman's house of the era and a smaller one at East Bilney. Much of the timber-framing of the houses of Little Walsingham dates to the sixteenth century. At Pulham Market the houses look a full century older but they had new chimneys in Elizabeth's reign as the standards of comfort for the ordinary man increased.

The sixteenth century is the first wherein the names of the ordinary men of Norfolk villages become known to us, and sometimes their wealth, at least in comparative terms, may be apparent too. Parish registers and tax returns are our sources. Parish registers began with the edict of Thomas Cromwell—the man who master-minded the destruction of the monasteries—that each parish should record the names of those baptised, those married and those buried within its precincts and those of the churchyard. Often, too, the volume was used to record events and other facts about the place. At Titchwell the transcript goes back to 1464. The actual register here begins in 1558. Twenty years earlier, Marsham register began and it has been transcribed and printed; it is complete to 1836. In all, fifty-two places have registers beginning in the first year of Cromwell's act. The parishes are scattered throughout the whole of Norfolk: Pulham Market, Pulham St Mary, Quidenham, Ringstead, Rockland St Peter and Runham are some. The communities differ. Terrington St John is a marshland village, Tittleshall-cum-Godwick is dominated by its lord, for this is the resting place of the Coke family. Thompson is in Breckland proper and Thruxton is small, out in the wilds, one of the lesser villages of Mitford Hundred. Thelveton belongs to the empty farmlands of South Norfolk. At Gressenhall, the first book of the parish register was lost until March 1900 and the record was thought to date only from 1720. The first book, begun in 1538, was in use until then. At Hunstanton the register also begins in 1538 but has no entries for the reign of Queen Mary (1553–8). There are often later gaps in the parish record: East Winch parish register does not begin until 1678 but the record from 1750 to 1759 is incomplete and those for other periods are missing completely. A Tudor beginning may be followed by a Stuart gap and many parishes have no record between 1642 and 1653. In that year a list was begun of the vital events, which was copied out on the restoration of Charles II to form in some cases the beginning of a new book. Hunworth is one such parish whose records begin in 1653; others are Letheringsett, Letton, Tacolneston, Thorpe-next-Haddiscoe and Wood Dalling. There are a few variants of this. In the marshland, Upwell begins in 1650 and Walpole St Andrew in 1654: earlier records here had been kept in the parish register of Walpole St Peter. At Mattishall and at Rockland St Mary the earliest record is of 1656 and at the latter the first fifty years of the parish register are in Latin. They are also in Latin in the early part of Surlingham register which begins in 1561, a year when fourteen other registers begin.

Three years earlier, on 17th November, the Princess Elizabeth succeeded her ill-fated half-sister as Queen of England. Late in her reign, in 1597, the queen decreed that the registers of each of the churches of her realm should be written out on good quality parchment from the first year of her reign. The registers of ninety Norfolk villages now begin in 1558. In all, half of the parishes of

Norfolk have a register which now begins a decade before Elizabeth's edict, and only forty-one of those have a commencing date of 1564 or later.

Parish registers had become well established by the time the other data about the people of Norfolk villages in the Age of the Visitations was available. Elizabethan England faced a number of external problems: the great Armada of 1588 was only the most celebrated of the threats. Ireland was always a curse; as my comments on royal arms will relate the Tudor Queen had little time for her other island. It devoured her treasury of money and her land of men. In 1569, 1574 and especially in 1577 listings were taken of men in each county by township. In 1581 the Queen did that rare act: she summoned a parliament to grant her money. For 1581 part of the subsidy assessments has been printed. They cover five of the hundreds of the county; muster rolls survive for fifteen hundreds out of the thirty-three the county had. Three of these hundreds coincide in both the muster rolls of 1577 and the subsidy of 1581. They are the hundreds of Mitford, Shropham and South Greenhoe which are respectively north-east, south and north-west of a fourth hundred, that of Wayland for which the 1577 muster roll is also extant. In general the 1577 listings are from the hundreds west of Norwich, excluding the north-west corner of the county. The exceptions are the records for North Erpingham Hundred and South Erpingham Hundred.

No parish church in Norfolk has a major collection of militia armour today, but in 1577 there was a longbow, a sheaf of arrows, a pike and a firearm at Gresham. Record was made of the arms and armour held by individuals here as in other parishes of North Erpingham Hundred; it was also made for Holt, North Greenhoe, and Eynesford Hundreds. No other record was taken of these; but for Guiltgross, Mitford and Shropham Hundred both armour and men are known for 1577 and in 1574 additionally for the first and the last. About the villages of much of the modern district of Breckland we are exceptionally well informed.

The emphasis has changed. No longer is the church the centre of the Norfolk village; the Age of the Visitations was secular in its aspirations and individualist in its outlook. The church was made to reflect the very changed atmosphere. At the heart of the world was the state. Henry VIII had made himself Defender of the Faith and Supreme Governor of the Church of England. Men came as much to worship the all-powerful machine as the older deity. At Ludham, St Catharine's Church expresses it well. The long, fifteenth-century arcades beneath a hammer-beam roof lead quite naturally to the screen of 1493 given by John and Cicily Salmon. Above the painted rood beam, itself a rare survival, the chancel arch is filled like the tympanum above a door. Here a painting on canvas, affixed to boards, stares at the worshipper, its message clear: Christ on the Cross died for men's sins, His mother, St Mary, and the disciple whom He loved, St John, acknowledge the Passion. It has been variously dated: the fifteenth century or the reign of Queen Mary (1553–8), herself an adherent to the Roman Catholic faith. At some stage the whole thing was hidden in the stairs to the rood loft, although the boards themselves were used for a new purpose. Norfolk has no royal arms of Henry VIII or of his sickly son, Edward VI, but for Elizabeth there are three surviving. At Ludham, now facing the altar not the congregation, a glorious blue expanse symbolized the power of the Tudor state, the heraldic achievement recorded their Welsh forbears.

Elizabeth I was a great queen; her progresses were legendary. She came to Kenninghall Place in 1578. The present Duke of Norfolk still owns this fragment of a then much larger courtyard house of rich red brick and a blue diaper. Her half-sister, Queen Mary, had spent most of the six long years of the reign of their half-brother, Edward VI, at this lonely spot, far away from the hurly-burly of the court. The house was new then in the late 1540s, four sides to a courtyard and attendant farm buildings. A generation later than the Princess Mary's stay, the people of Kenninghall felt the need to demonstrate their loyalty to the resplendent Elizabethan state. One wonders how the entourage of the queen would have managed to squeeze into what is quite a small church by universal standards although among the largest of the churches of Norfolk villages. On entry, the queen regnant and dominant would have seen the red chargings of English lion and Welsh dragon supporting quartered lions of Plantagenet, three of gold against a red field, and fleurs de lys of France, gold against an insipid blue. It stood then to fill the chancel arch, and not as now relegated to a position in the north aisle above the former parclose (or chapel) screen. In her entry, Elizabeth would have sense the affection the lively painting transmits even today, four hundred years later.

A stature of greatness is seen in the third of the royal arms from a Norfolk village church which date as early as Elizabeth: those at Tivetshall St Margaret. If that at Ludham is elegant and that at Kenninghall playful, the creation at Tivetshall of 1587 in setting and in size reflects the power of Elizabethan England. Again it fills the tympanum between nave and chancel; it reflects another assumed accomplishment of Elizabethan England: the ability to read. Beneath the heraldry, beneath the protestation of loyalty—"God save our Queene Elizabeth"—there are the awful words of the ten commandments.

A lot of churches have commandment boards. At Caister, two boards hanging either side of the tower arch have Moses and Aaron flanking the inscription. The arrangement is late seventeenth century in style. Of later date is the board at Burnham Overy, where four panels, occupying a space five metres by two metres, record the commandments, the creed and the Lord's Prayer. It was erected in 1747. A full century earlier are the boards in the church at Terrington St Clement, dated to 1635, on which the creed and the Lord's Prayer are written. These fill the east walls of the south and north transepts respectively but the two boards giving the ten commandments have not survived. In Shipdham church those of 1630 were made as part of the tympanum of the chancel arch. The royal arms are dated 1661 but are convincingly argued to be contemporary with the commandments; as a tympanic rendering they may even be Elizabethan in origin. The heraldry is Stuart and in part reflects the date of the commandment board. This board now hangs on the west wall of the nave, opposite its original setting, while the commandment board rests beneath the hefty braces of the second bay of the north aisle. Only the carved bosses suggest the interior of a church. Shipdham church has another feature of the Age of the Visitations. Atop the tower is a lantern, certainly there in 1815 when it was drawn by Dawson Turner. It is of wood, covered with lead. A copy was made for the Victorian restoration of nearby Necton church.

The Stuart monarchs, collectively and individually, were less confident as kings than Elizabeth I. Their arms reflect their less assured position: the fire of the dragon is replaced by the meekness of the unicorn. Scotland not Wales was their ancestral home and the old arms became as at Wilby, of after 1633, merely the first and fourth quarters; red lion rampant for Scotland and golden harp for Ireland respectively occupy the second and third quarters. The size and the shape too have changed. The tympanic treatment at Shipdham is unusual. Now it is a board, either square or oblong. It may be large; nobody would call the arms of James II at Great Snoring and at Little Snoring puny. The adjective could be applied to the miniscule board above the chancel arch, not within it, which the visitor might almost miss in the church of Winterton-on-Sea. It belongs to the reign of Charles I.

The reign of his father, James I, left ten of these achievements in the villages of Norfolk: dated 1610 at Blo' Norton, 1619 at Marham, and 1620 at Tilney St Lawrence. There are updated examples at Helhoughton, Hillborough, Kimberley, Marsham and Tacolneston, plus one dated 1762 at Moulton but bearing the motto "Exurgat Deus" used by James I. Fragmentary is the example at Frenze. The achievements of Charles I date essentially to the 1630s: at Riddlesworth in 1632 (repainted in 1666) and North Creake in 1635. Undated are those at Gorleston, a magnificent example this subsequently repainted in 1664, at Narford, very faded but still in position over the chancel arch, and at Pulham St Mary the Virgin. Three others at least of this reign have been painted over and reused. At Kenninghall the second arms, a square board, seems to belong to the eighteenth century. The lettering says "G R" but the initial letter is altered from a "C" and without the qualifying numeral, the father rather than the son would seem to be indicated. As at Shipdham, one would guess, the old arms at Dickleburgh were repainted and dated 1662 after the restoration of Charles II: the surround suggests his father. A much later repainting is that of 1745 carried out at Reepham. Again the heraldry is Stuart and probably of Charles I.

No king was the focus of attention in the 1650s but with the restoration of Charles II in 1660, the practice of placing royal arms in churches was resumed and made compulsory. One Norfolk village Great Witchingham, was given a new set in 1660 by Oliver le Neve but no donor is recorded for the exactly contemporary set at East Harling. The set of 1661 at Toft Monks is one of two in the church; the other arms are those of George II and dated 1745. A score are recognizable as of Charles II but for the reign of James

II two alone stand. The earlier, at Little Snoring, dated to the three months when 1686 overlapped 1687 (depending on whether 1st January or 25th March was the first day of the year), is probably the first painting of the board. That of a year later, at nearby Great Snoring, is perhaps a reuse of an earlier board. Yet both share the ebullient cheekiness of the village craftsman, the same plump animals, the same faces with the lips of the lion being licked. At Great Snoring there is a seventeenth-century commandment board too, a more sober piece a Trinity between two panels of words which have the last things—Heaven, Death, Hell and Judgement—beside them, flanked by representations probably of Moses and Aaron. Once this stood behind the altar, now it is opposite the south door; the royal arms are above the makeshift entrance lobby to the same door. Less usual in a village church is the contemporary Dutch painting of "Christ Healing".

Like those of Elizabeth's reign, the royal arms set up in village churches in the reign of Charles II have a political significance. Those at Quidenham are carved in wood and unpainted. The changed material for the expression of loyalty, itself, reflects a change in the significance of the device. Already the work had become a vehicle for artistry. Three generations later a professional heraldic artist could be employed at Eccles, while at Old Buckenham the same arms of George II were painted by a man unskilled in the trade. Here a local man, one suspects the village wainwright, had his fancy and made the lion and the unicorn plump, like fat beasts in the fields, with faces that laugh a little. More than one notable in the two hundred or more villages of Norfolk with a royal arms of any date beyond the 1660s has found himself mocked Sunday by Sunday as the parishioners saw what one of their fellows had made of their squire.

It is surely not without significance that no royal arms remain hung in a Norfolk village church which has become the store house of the effigies of the great of the late seventeenth century and beyond. Their ways were too powerful. That power survived their death. The medieval monumental brass took up little space and that only on the floor.

The Age of the Visitations changed how men thought about the use of the church by the dead. They wished to be remembered, and to be seen to be remembered. East Harling is a large village, one might almost say a "village town", but the process of acquisition is aptly demonstrated here. Harling, Chamberlain and Lovell are the families involved. In 1435, Sir Robert Harling died. He was laid against the south wall of the south aisle at the east end beside the altar. He had given a screen to the aisle and this marks off part as the family chapel. Sir William Chamberlain, first husband of Anne, only child of Sir Robert Harling, lies buried under a chantry on the north side of the chancel, not quite, one might add, within the sanctuary area. The daughter and her successive husbands rebuilt the church. Yet in the sixteenth century the land in the village passed to the Lovell family. Two early members appropriated for themselves places beside the sanctuary: Sir Francis Lovell, who died in 1551, to the north without any inscription, and his son, Sir Thomas, to the south. The latter died in 1567 but his son, also Sir Thomas Lovell, made no pretence at restraint. His monument—it is more than a tomb—fills half the wall of the Harling chapel in the south aisle. The man and his wife, Dame Alice, lie on a huge box protected by columns and by obelisks. Only the lettering detracts from this early Jacobean monument which retains its original paint. It dates to 1604.

East Harling church has the full range of monuments of the Age of the Visitations and before. The Felbriggs and the Windhams in Felbrigg church will be noted later but these are in latten to men and women who died between 1351 and 1608. Stone was not used here until after the restoration of Charles II. The series in the parish church of Blickling again is mainly monumental brasses, the earliest of James of Helveston (died 1378) and the latest to Anne Wood who died in 1612, but one effigy is dated to 1582 and Sir Edward Clere, a contemporary, lacks dates and effigy on his tomb chest. Yet the great series of sculptures are few. One group stands out, the Bedingfeld monuments in the chapel of Oxborough church. The chapel dates to after 1514 when Margaret Bedingfeld's will directed that she be laid in the chapel yet to be built. There are two terracotta tombs here, neither dated exactly but in style belonging to around 1525. A later monument is to Sir Henry Bedingfeld, servant of Mary Tudor and custodian of her sister, who died in 1583; for him alabaster and Corinthian columns.

Sir Robert Southwell had died two full decades earlier; he lies recumbent in Wood Rising church, yet of the style that has good claim to be the best type of English funerary monument there may at most be a couple of dozen in Norfolk villages. A fair proportion of these belong to a single sculptor's work, that of Nicholas Stone. His predecessors were few. The only real family group is of the Corbetts in Sprowston church, of 1559, of 1607 and of 1617, with other men from other families commemorated in pieces recording deaths in 1610 and the late seventeenth and eighteenth centuries.

The gentry of Norfolk in the Age of the Visitations were not few. The collected visitations of 1563, 1589 and 1613 record over three hundred families, yet in a hundred Norfolk churches one may see only a handful of monuments. There are the single monuments to new men, those whose lands were amassed by themselves: Sir Edward Barkham at South Acre, Edmund Reve of 1647 at Long Stratton—a late piece this—Miles Branthwaite at Hethel of 1612, and Sir Wymond Carye at Snettisham, also of 1612. Another death of that year was Sir Henry Sidney of Little Walsingham, a younger son but scion of a family established in trade on the north Norfolk coast during the great Queen's reign, who by the purchase of land turned themselves into gentry and in James I's reign achieved a knighthood. Sir Henry is below his wife but in front of her; Edmund Reve, already noted, looks down from above and behind his wife with a kindly smile, but William Peck, who died in 1635, at Spixworth stares out into space from his couch above his wife. These two have shrouds, as does Thomas Marsham, who died in 1638, at Stratton Strawless.

Some men were distinctly from families not new in the Age of the Visitations and for them the best alone was reserved. Sir Clement Spelman was the fifth generation to be interred in Narborough church when he died in 1607; and two generations have later monuments. The family were already established in the parish before the Reformation but Sir John Spelman, who died in 1545, was among those who sent that good man Sir Thomas More to his death. His reward for faithful service was land at Narborough, formerly monastic. He was commemorated in brass like his father; so was his son, another John, and a grandson, yet another John; but Sir Clement was robed with his lady in alabaster, following the style of his day.

The Pastons had no need to fawn upon a king's pleasure. Despite inactivity in Kett's Rebellion, they could command more loyalty in Norfolk villages than any prince, perhaps even more than a queen, although the Tudor state became more powerful as its century progressed. The earlier monuments are at Paston, but three are without names, one of which was transported to the church from Broomham Priory. A later Paston, Sir William, is buried away; his monument by John Key is in North Walsham church. Dying in 1608, he founded Paston Grammar School in the local town. Yet two monuments in Paston are later. They are by Nicholas Stone, as is another in Oxnead church. The same sculptor did three others in village churches: an early work of 1617 at Emneth to Sir Thomas Hewer, and two contemporary with the Paston tombs. They are both to members of the more newly emergent Coke family. Sir Edward Coke, Lord Chief Justice, and husband of a Paston, died in 1634. He is commemorated in black and white marble and white recumbent effigy with Tuscan columns. No price is known for this but the fame of Stone had spread. In 1617 his price was £95 for the Hewer monument. On the tomb at Paston of Dame Katherine Paston, who died in 1629, Stone wrote in his diary: "I was very extraordinarily entertained and paid for it £340." He did this in alabaster and with a semi-reclining effigy. Yet three years later for Sir Edmund Paston he could create a classical monument, not out of place a century later. In stone and black marble the knight had a plain urn. Another Paston, Lady Katherine, four years later still was commemorated by a bust in Oxnead church. This church contains the superb alabaster piece to Sir Clement Paston. He died in 1597, a year before his daughter, Sir Edward Coke's wife, who is also commemorated in alabaster, kneeling with her children. But the latter, in Tittleshall church, like her father's monument at Oxnead, represents a different tradition from the sculptor's art.

The Pastons were great builders. They took over Caister Castle in 1459 and lived there until 1599. Some time before they had begun the house at Oxnead, but of this little remains; it was described as "in utmost ruins" already in 1744, a mere thirteen years after the estate had been sold to Admiral Anson. At Paston there survives only the great barn and from Drayton Lodge a fragment still stands; it had a brick newel stair. Others in Norfolk occur in Upwell Rectory, Oxburgh Hall and the tower of Newton Flotman church.

At the beginning of the Age of the Visitations the whole context of worship changed. The Reformation removed much that had been familiar; in its place came the Book of Common Prayer, the first compiled in glorious prose by Thomas Cranmer for Edward VI, the second that of 1662 used without a break until quite recently. Elizabeth took the decisive step that sacrament rather than office would remain the distinctive feature of English church services. It is only with the Victorians that Mattins and Evensong assumed any prominence. At the same time there came another of those orgies of destruction that have marked the history of the Norfolk village church. Jacobean woodwork was their victim. Elizabethan silver was allowed to survive. There are pieces earlier than 1567. All Saints', Thornage, has a chalice given by John Butes and Margaret his wife in 1456; he died in 1477. The paten too is early, dating to 1563. The chalice of St John's, Hoveton, was made the year before this but not given to the church until 1824. Earlier, but still within Elizabeth's reign, if it is English, is the chalice of All Saints', Hethel: it may be Flemish work of 1532. From Edward VI's years is the chalice and paten of St Mary's, Hunstanton, then, of course, still a village. The great change comes in the 1560s. No fewer than 275 churches in the county have plate of 1567–8; there are twenty-eight from the three years previous and fifteen from the three years following. To take a single letter of the alphabet for the examples: at Mattishall Burgh and Mulbarton chalice and paten are of 1567–8; the chalice at Morningthorpe is undated but Elizabethan, as is the paten at Morton-on-the-Hill; the chalice at Mundham was made in 1567. In the villages of Broadland and North Norfolk, there is the same array of Elizabethan silver: Martham has a chalice and cover of 1567–8, and undated are the chalice and paten of Mautby and Marsham. Much of this silver, like the chalice of Metton of 1567 and the paten of All Saints', Mundesley, of the same year, was made in Norwich. Norfolk villages patronized their local craftsmen both in Elizabeth's time and in that of her Stuart successors. Morley St Peter has a Norwich-made chalice of 1637 and Morley St Botolph one of 1664. For West Norfolk, King's Lynn was (and is) the centre. At Middleton, there is the fine chalice and cover of 1632, made not ten miles away.

There are two contrasting strains in religious expression in the early seventeenth century. Both find more than an echo in Norfolk villages. In 1559 Elizabeth had permitted the removal of stone altars; five years later a decree required "that the parish provide a decent table standing on a frame for the Communion Table". West Winch and Clenchwarton have tables of Elizabeth's latter years, Scarning and Salle are among those with Stuart tables. Others include Scole and Scottow, Shimpling and Sisland, Great Snoring and Sparham, Strumpshaw and Swanton Morley. The richly carved table of St Margaret's, Swannington, is dated 1635 and the rails enclosing the table of St Nicholas's, Salthouse, belong to three years later. St Botolph's, Shingham, had pulpit, reading desk and altar rails all of the first generation of the seventeenth century. Archbishop Laud in 1634 sought to enclose the altar within the chancel. He ordered that: "the rail be made before the Communion table reaching across from the north wall to the south wall, near one yard in height, so thick with pillars that the dogs may not get in."

Turned balusters and posts are the hallmark of the earliest rails. St Helen's, Ranworth, and St Peter's, Lingwood, are churches with examples. At St Peter's, Reymerston, the altar rails are Flemish work; at Taverham and at Little Melton, the villagers made do with an old screen. Seventeenth-century churchwardens in poor country parishes were not going to be put to too great an expense.

Contemporary with Laud and his man at Norwich, Bishop Matthew Wren, another tradition was growing up in the Church of England. Preaching was becoming all the rage.

Pulpits are found earlier than the seventeenth century. Painted panels adorn those of the fifteenth century at Castle Acre, Horsham St Faith and Burnham Norton. The contemporary pulpits of Heydon, Cawston and South Creake are traceried in their decoration. Paint can still be discerned on the last-named as it can on the one at Burlingham St Edmund. Here they put a backboard and a canopy to the earlier work some time during the early seventeenth century. At Salle they went further and encased a wineglass pulpit with reader's desk and clerk's seat, a remarkable piece which speaks of the affection which men felt for their parish church.

Elsewhere they were less ambitious. At Shipdham, perhaps reusing an earlier base and certainly incorporating an earlier top, the churchwardens provided an octagonal structure, simple in its panels restrained in its feeling. It is light years away from the earlier creations. In the reigns of both James I and his son, Charles

I, abundant provision was made for preaching. The pulpit at Beeston St Mary belongs to 1592. There is a prayer desk of 1619 at Moulton St Mary and a contemporary Jacobean pulpit, undated but clearly part of the same design. At North Elmham, Francis Field, the parish clerk, was paid a pound for carving the pulpit in 1614 and twelve years later received a further £4 3s 4d for finishing it. There is a date of 1626 on the backboard. The pulpit at Walpole St Peter, dated 1620, retains its tester and both back panel and tester survive with that of Thwaite St Mary, dated 1624. There are geometrical patterns on the panels of the pulpit at Wiggenhall St Germans, dated 1631; the iron hour-glass stand is attached. But the pulpit at Thornham, also of 1631, is plain. Of a year later is the pulpit of Edingthorpe, but this church has a reader's desk of 1587 built up from panels roughly put together to form a square. It is a long way from the sheer glory of the pulpit of All Saints', Necton, dated to 1636. It neatly complements the roof and above is one of the best clerestories in Norfolk: eight windows each of three lights. Arch braces alternate with hammer-beams, but these are really brackets for the angels with traceried spandrels. Richly gilded, the whole looks down and, like all these roofs, defied the vandalism that struck England less than a decade after the pulpit at Necton was carved.

Norwich Cathedral was where the iconoclasts struck first with a frenzy which dismayed many who sympathized with their motives. Their brutality later generations can only condemn. Men as diverse in their opinions and in their later stances as Sir Harmon l'Estrange of Hunstanton and Thomas Windham of Felbrigg hurried to ensure their parishes would not have the same visitations of vice and vindictiveness. The l'Estrange family had been long established in the county. The brasses of Felbrigg church commemorate an earlier and unrelated set of owners. However, Windham deserves our thanks for keeping the monuments sacrosanct from what he described as "the detestable fury and the very odious oppression."

Another change came as men, no more odious to our taste than many who remained, were removed from their parishes. Nathaniel Gill went from Burgh-next-Aylsham in 1651, defiant, uncompromising with that tyrannical regime which came after Charles I's execution. He had written Latin verses in the parish register since his institution in 1638 and he went on using the ageless rites of the Church of England. His parishioners respected him and aided his courage. When defiance was quashed and he was forced to retire to Bungay, he took the parish register with him. After the restoration of Charles II, Nathaniel Gill came back to Burgh as rector and he had no doubt of his position: "Nathaniel Gill (after seventeen years sequestration, by traitors, rebels, Anabaptists, Quakers, and Presbyterians) was restored to his rectory of Burgh and preached on Christmas Day 1660."

One need have no doubt as to who these men were who sought to rule England's hearts. A Norfolk rector described them well: "Parliament rogues, roundheads, rebels to the King and traitors," wrote Richard Plummer of Sustead and Alby who refused to contribute to the cost of the rebellion. There were Royalist clergy by the score in Norfolk villages; men whose quiet dignity and courage speak volumes for their independence of mind, their fearless spirit, their straightforward idealism. John Lewthwaite of Rockland St Peter and Stow Bedon spoke for them all when he said: "We have a merciful King, which is forced to take up arms to fight to maintain the true Protestant religion."

Sequestrated clergy, deprived of their livings and often denied the livelihood of being schoolmasters, were to be found all over the county. In the north-east corner, the villages produced many who stood out for the King. Thomas Thexton of Trunch and Gimingham, Richard Howes of Knapton, Thomas Campbell of Swafield, Thomas Reeve of Aldborough and Colby, and Robert le Neve of Scottow. A fifth of the income, at the very most, was allowed for the maintenance of their families. It was a pittance less than that of a labourer.

The chains of theocratic dictatorship did not survive the evil genius who signed first the death warrant of a king. Miles Corbett of Sprowston, too, had sat in judgement that day in January 1649; in 1662 he paid the penalty he had exacted of a king. By then it was twenty-five years since men had first refused to pay taxes without parliamentary sanction and as old Sir Jacob Astley, a royalist, had remarked: "You have now done your work, boys, and may go to play unless you will fall out amongst yourselves."

Those in revolt did tear themselves asunder as families in Norfolk villages, low as well as high, were rent by the Civil War. The Astleys were among them, for Sir Jacob's daughter had married her cousin, Edward, and the latter supported parliament not the

King. Their son, another Sir Jacob, raised the present Melton Hall at Melton Constable, when the troubles were over. Men in the 1660s vowed never again to cast asunder those bonds which held man to man. They had closed ranks by the time the 1664 visitation came. The eighteenth-century world which followed reflected the desire for order; the Age of the Visitations had been too full of trouble and generated too much strife. It had vigour but it needed the calm to follow.

V

Norfolk Husbandry

SEVEN generations lived and died in the villages of Norfolk between the last of the visitations (1664) and the accession of Queen Victoria (1837). At the heart of the villages was change, the massive change historians have termed the agricultural revolution. At the heart of this was change initiated in Norfolk, a four-course rotation of crops called "Norfolk husbandry". It may serve as a title for my chapter surveying both the changes in Norfolk villages between the late seventeenth century and the mid-nineteenth-century and the stability too. The word "husbandry" implies stability as well as change: men lived and died by the harvest. When it failed they died, at least in the early years of the period, for no greater reason than the sheer lack of food to fill their stomachs. In the last years of the eighteenth century, recorded in immense depth by the Rev. James Woodforde, Rector of Weston Longueville, there was famine too but men did not die of the harsh, brutal cause, starvation.

The eighteenth century has many images: that for Norfolk and its villages it was a farming century there can be no doubt. Yet even for this most agricultural of counties it was much more. Norfolk abounds in grand houses. There are the well-known ones like Holkham Hall and Houghton Hall. There are destroyed ones like Gunton Park, gutted by a fire of 1882 and never rebuilt. There are the little-known ones like Langley Park, Kimberley Hall and Wolterton Hall. They convey that sense of elegance for which the eighteenth century is justly famed.

Yet for the villages of the county, these six houses have another significance. There just is not a village except, as at Houghton,

Holkham and Kimberley, one created after the park was laid out. There is a round tower from the church of the former village at Wolterton; there is not even that at Langley. Here a cross stands where the parishes of Langley with Hardley, Chedgrave, Thurton and Carleton St Peter meet. The slender square shaft with four saints on pedestals once graced, it is thought, the centre of Langley village but this was removed for the park. A village within the grounds of the great park would never have suited the creators of eighteenth-century landscapes. Their view of elegance demanded vistas unhindered by houses, views encompassed by grazing and trees. As any visitor to Holkham is well aware wheat is grown within the acres: at 2,150 hectares (5,313 acres) the parish is among the largest in the county and nearly all of it is park. Yet in this, the largest park in Norfolk, the view is of sheep grazing within a tree-lined horizon, broken only on the west by water.

There is a village at Holkham, out beside the entrance to the park on the coast road. Yet the church is not near: Its tower pokes out from the trees on a rise the other side of the lake. The present village at Holkham is not eighteenth century. The original village, rebuilt between 1744 and 1759, was replaced in the 1890s by a series of semi-detached houses forming a drive to the north gate. The real entrance to Holkham Hall is from the south, at New Holkham, over the hill and down the avenue, past the Obelisk of 1729.

The old village was still there when the Obelisk and the contemporary temple were built. It stood between the house and the lake. When the village was moved the outlying fields of the parish were made into four large farms: Branthill Farm and Quarles Farm are outside the park, Longlands Farm and Howe Hill within it. Such is the effect of an early enclosure.

What Thomas Coke, first Earl of Leicester, attempted at Holkham, a contemporary, Sir Robert Walpole, did at another Norfolk village. There was a village at Houghton before the park was made; it stood perhaps again near the church. It was gone by 1740. The parish register of Houghton notes that the foundations for the first houses of the new town were dug on 4th July 1729. Here the contemporary village remains: two rows of five houses. There were almshouses and two larger farmhouses. The latter front the road to West Rudham, but the rest of the village extends the avenue of trees approaching the gates of the park. Here is the eighteenth-century view of order, in whitewashed brick, resplendent on a sunny day, delightful to look at, calm and peaceful. It is part of the image the eighteenth century wished to project of itself.

Another, slightly later, creation of that image is the village at Heydon. The house is Elizabethan, the park a creation of Henry Dynne, a minor functionary of Elizabeth's entourage. Here the house was refurbished in 1797 when the houses, both terraces and pairs surrounding the village green and the street leading to it, were built. They have central gables to the pediments and severe fenestration but in a light red brick to which eye most readily responds. To break the monotony other dwellings are in yellow brick but of the same style.

The villages of Holkham, Houghton and Wolterton now are not where their medieval predecessors were. In place of the latter great parks appeared. Philip Yorke, later second Earl of Hardwicke, and husband of Jemima, the Marchioness Grey, kept a diary of his travels round Norfolk in 1750. At Houghton he was impressed:

> We had the opportunity of seeing the plantations and the park. The former are of vast extent, not less in the whole circuit than 13 miles, with serpentine ridings cut through them, and form beautiful thick cover to that wild barren country. The park is regularly planted, with some fine oaks near the house which Lord Orford used pleasantly to call his schoolmasters, because they taught him trees would grow there; and indeed trees of all kinds thrive extremely well in this soil. The deer park is 6 miles round, besides what is kept in the farm.

He had been to Raynham that morning, but the weather was less kind to the earl and his marchioness—he always called her Lady Grey. Here, round a house a century older, he saw a park:

> The chief beauty of it seems to consist in groves of old trees dispersed about the different parts of it, but we thought the lawns too naked and the whole but indifferently kept. There is a lake of 36 acres near the house, the banks of which are in bad order, and the water concealed injudiciously by hedgerows and underwood in one part of it.

The great of the eighteenth century were expected to be discerning patrons, knowledgeable about their surroundings: Hardwicke and his wife were seeking ideas for improving the grounds of the Bedfordshire seat of Lady Grey, Wrest Park. Trees were expected in the eighteenth century. Away to the east, the visitors viewed two seats. Again both park and garden drew Philip Yorke's attentive eye. At Wolterton, he saw Horatio Walpole's house in grounds laid out by Charles Bridgeman:

> The ground about the house is 80 acres within a sunk fence, which is laid out in open groves of oak and beech, some of them old trees, but the greatest part planted by Mr Walpole, and all look very thriving. To the front of the house lies a large irregular piece of water consisting of 15 acres, with a terrace and a plantation round it. The park is a small one, but has in it several rises and falls in the ground which are picturesque.

Blickling Hall, then well over a century old, is south of the River Bure. This, too, the Yorkes visited but Philip's comments were less complimentary about new plantations which were "not so well managed as they might have been and rather too much crowded".

If the eighteenth century demanded great parks, it demanded also houses sufficient to fill these expanses with their lakes and their rides. Pride of place must go to Holkham Hall. Philip Yorke is again worth quoting, for he went there before it was finished. He was enthusiastic:

> The house is now in building, and if ever finished perhaps the finest in England. The general plan of it is a corps de logis with a pavilion at each corner. The west pavilion is entirely finished, and contains the private apartments of Lord and Lady Leicester, which consists of five rooms with an anteroom to that used by his lordship. The rooms in general are small, but highly ornamented and gilded. There are two rooms in the attic for Lord Coke and a winter dining-parlour below stairs. The shell of the corps de logis is up but not entirely covered in; it is a most beautiful building. A portico projects from the south front of the house, supported by six Corinthian pillars in front and three in depth. The ascent to it will be by a flight of steps on each side of it, which will lead to the principal floor. The north front has five large Venetian windows in it, which have a very good effect. You come in at once upon the great hall, which is a cube of 46 ft; at the upper end is a circular recess from whence is to be the ascent into the salon. The whole of this corps de logis will consist of fourteen rooms, one of which is to be a gallery of 60 ft.

Philip Yorke's taste is almost the conventional view: admiring, nearly one might add, obsequious. Yet there is another view: the eighteenth century had a sense of its own splendour, a gargantuan taste for its own grandeur. To enter the stone hall by William Kent of 1734–53 is to feel the stamp of authority born quite simply of acres. Holkham Hall seems just too big, too grand. The setting is superb, yet against a drab day the yellow brick of the exterior exhibits a coldness that is frightening. How much warmer is the red brick of Raynham Hall, a century earlier, and for that matter how much more sensible is Raynham as a house. Perhaps it is small wonder that the family chose to live in a pavilion at Holkham.

Quite how these houses were used is brought out by Philip Yorke. The visitors from Bedfordshire stayed at Wolterton Hall from 20th to 24th July 1750. The husband described the arrangements there:

> The house is square, and consists of a rustic, a first floor (where the best apartments lie), and attic and garrets. The family live in the rustic where are four good plain rooms, the dining parlour, the drawing room, the study and the breakfast room. The rest are for servants. On the first floor are eight rooms, a hall, salon, drawing room, dining parlour, and two apartments consisting of a bedchamber and a dressing room. They are all handsomely furnished, adorned with marble chimney pieces (and hung with the best Brussels tapestry), stucco ceilings and friezes. The attic consists of lodging rooms, which are very good ones.

Horatio Walpole, who built this house between 1727 and 1741, evidently liked his food and kept the dining-room for general use in a sensible place, adjacent to the kitchen.

The grand rooms their owners felt could clearly be left to the visitors who were there at Holkham in force already in 1772. These rooms are settings for collections of paintings and at Holkham of statues too. The taste for statuary is older than the eighteenth century. The Pastons, in the early eighteenth century Earls of Yarmouth and on their last legs as a landed family, had employed Nicholas Stone to create a classical splendour at Oxnead Hall. One alone of the series survives: a Hercules of 1632 and a contemporary fountain are now at Blickling Hall.

Other eighteenth-century houses are homes rather than showpieces. The conventional houses of the landed gentry, whether the village squire or the man who had bought an estate, were no more than a single pavilion of Holkham Hall. Salle Park was built in the same year, 1761, as Holkham was finished. Edward Hase was his own architect and used red brick. Some men used professional architects. In the latter part of the century Sir John Soane was much employed: at Westgate Hall, Burnham Market, in 1783, at Saxlingham Parsonage in the following year, and at Letton Hall between 1785 and 1788. He also designed the lodges to Langley Park, about 1790. They have a charm which is not so easily discerned at the house—an older creation, by Matthew Brettingham in the 1740s and completed before 1755. Soane is more refined, more delicate and even if Shotesham Hall, of about 1785, is large, the Music Room of Earsham Hall, a separate building set away from the house in the grounds, reflects the atmosphere of the subscription concert, echoes the feel of the years when Mozart was no longer a child prodigy: one can almost hear the strings of the G minor quintet.

An echo of this refinement permeated down into the villages. The individual façades may have dates more properly to be ascribed to the nineteenth rather than the eighteenth century. The intention is the same: a brick house, or a brick façade to an older timber-framed or flint house, signifying a new flourish of wealth, a desire to seem in the fashion. Often it is successful, and if without too much of the classical overtones as most of the later examples are, the village is much improved at least as the eighteenth century understood that word. This most definitely is the world of James Woodforde, its faces alternately dignified and genteel and if not sordid then at least squalid and certainly poor. The fees for churching a woman, after the birth of her child, are remitted, the wedding fee given by the man is handed to the woman after the nuptials have been solemnized, the deaths from smallpox and from violent fevers of men not yet in their prime, the frequent burials of children almost new born; these are the marks of a society not yet affluent. James Woodforde at Weston Longueville recorded the poor of his village in detail as vivid as his own dinners. A single one of the latter may suffice. On Friday, 8th April 1796, the rector and his guests consumed

> a fine cod's head and shoulders, boiled, and oyster sauce, peas-soup, ham and two boiled chickens, and a fine saddle of mutton roasted, potatoes, cauliflower, broccoli, and cucumber. Second

> course: a roast duck, macaroni, a sweet batter pudding and currant jelly, blancmange, and raspberry puff. Dessert: oranges, almonds and raisins, nuts, and dried apples, beef juice. Port and sherry wines, porter, strong beer and small.

Almost a fortnight later the good rector and his niece were guests at another's table, Mr Mellish at East Tuddenham. They were equally royally fed on

> salmon boiled and shrimp sauce, some white soup, saddle of mutton roasted and cucumber etc., lamb's fry, tongue, breast of veal, ragoued, rice pudding, the best part of a rump of beef stewed immediately the salmon was removed. Second course: a couple of spring chicken, roasted sweetbreads, jellies, macaroni, frilled oysters, two small crabs, and a made dish of eggs.

The next sentence provides a contrast back to the world of other men:

> No kind of pastry, no wheat flour made use of an even the melted butter thickened with wheatmeal, and the bread all brown wheatmeal with one part in four of barley flour. The bread was well made and ate very well indeed, may we never eat worse.

Yet many in Norfolk in Parson Woodforde's day ate far worse than this, for prices rose at the end of the century to levels describable only as bordering those of a famine. Added to this the weather turned nasty. The last years of the eighteenth century were marked by winters of extreme severity. James Woodforde's record is contemporary; his account prosaic of the difficult years when the snow lay deep upon the ground. At Weston church service was not always held, especially in February, and frosts marked April more than once. The entries in the diary for Tuesday, 2nd April, and Wednesday, 3rd April 1799, accurately reflect the world:

> Bitter cold again today, hard frost, but less wind. There being but few sound turnips, the poor stock such as bullocks, cows, sheep etc. are shockingly distressed, few farmers have scarce anything to give them. Scarce ever known such distressed times for stock of all kinds, nothing growing, no vegetation, everything almost dead in the gardens, beans and peas etc. almost all gone dead. It is grievous to behold how every vegetable is hurt—not even a daisy or any kind of flower seen. What a dismal dreary aspect have we at present.
>
> Very severe frosts still continue, bitter cold indeed. Every kind of

> vegetable almost destroyed by the frost. Turnips all froze—alas poor stock. Peas and beans sown in gardens, almost all gone. Such severe, cold weather of so long continuance was scarce known in the memory of man.

It went on, for in the May of that year the rector sold a neighbour hay for his beasts, Mr Girling "being greatly distressed for food for his sheep and cattle, the season continuing on so very cold and wet". It was not until 8th June that year that the rector could record seeing "all vegetation in the quickest growth and in the most flourishing state".

James Woodforde lived a more elevated life than his parishioners, yet among his pleasures there were similarities with those of the majority of his flock: the smuggled tub of rum, the coursed hare, the home-brewed barrel of beer. Their food was different from his. If he for a solitary dinner with his niece, Nancy, who was his housekeeper, could eat boiled tongue and mashed potatoes together with turnips and loin of veal roasted, they for their part had perhaps only the turnips and bread. Yet despite their poverty, it was less than it had been at the beginning of the eighteenth century.

The enthusiasts for enclosure, like Arthur Young and William Marshall, claimed it was due to improved farming methods. Historians have differed on the exact contribution made by the so-called agricultural revolution. Certainly the introduction of turnips by Viscount Townsend in the 1720s brought improved feed for cattle which meant that they could be kept over the winter. Townsend from his seat at Raynham Park took a critical look at the old three-field system of agriculture. As sole landowner of the parish he was able to impose an improved system on his tenants and on his home farm. Abolishing the fallow every third year meant improved yields from the soil; introducing the four-course rotation—in its basic form, wheat, root crop, barley, clover—brought higher yields too. The system was developed and modified. When Arthur Young came to investigate the agriculture of the country in 1802, he found five- and six-course rotations in practice. East Norfolk had a five-shift system with a crop of barley between the wheat and the root crop of the four-course. It was found at Caister, at Ludham, at Reeps and at Martham. The marshland was different, but again with a five-shift system. At Terrington, oats were used and potatoes, while fallow persisted at

Walpole. In the north-west, the deserted village of Egmere was ploughed to a six-course: turnips, barley, seeds for two years, tares and wheat. It thrilled Arthur Young: "What a noble spectacle is this farm! 300 acres of turnips, 300 of barley, 600 of seeds, 300 of tares and 300 of wheat: 1800 acres arable, the crops luxuriant, and much the greater part of the farm very clean."

Mr Purdis of Egmere and Viscount Townsend at Raynham were fortunate; their farms were compact and together in a single spread of land. Other men farmed area separated widely by holdings of their fellows. During the eighteenth century a great movement was afoot to change the pattern of land holding in each village and to make the farms more compact. Arthur Young was among the protagonists. No less than 120 of the 530 pages of *General View of the Agriculture of the County of Norfolk* are devoted to the topic. When Young wrote in 1804 the process was barely a third of the way through its course. There are 286 enclosure acts for the villages and towns of Norfolk whose details are of more than passing interest. A handful date to before the reign of George III: Stokesby (1721), Oxborough (1724), Great Bircham (1739), Watlington (1749), Brancaster (1755) and Swanton Morley (1755). There is a steady trickle of parishes applying to parliament for an act in the years before 1790: Snettisham in 1762, North Tuddenham in 1764, Scarning in 1765, Little Ellingham and Carleton Forehoe and Kimberley in 1766, and Shernborne in 1767. Both Fincham and Roudham applied in 1772 and six parishes secured acts in 1774. They were Weeting, Tottington and Barton Bendish, each of which has an individual act, while Beetly, Great Bittering and Gressenhall have an act which covers all three parishes. Five acts were passed in 1777, for Crownthorpe, Little Cressingham, Carleton Rode, Felthorpe, and Wreningham, but only that for Tacolneston in 1778. Those of Woodbastwick and Dersingham date to 1779. Whereas there are five acts for 1780 and four in 1781, the remainder of the 1780s are blank except for the Ashill Act of 1785, that for Titchwell in 1786 and those for the Walpole parishes and Banham in 1789. Acts had been passed for Foulden, Grimston, Heacham, Tottenhill and jointly for Salthouse and Kelling in 1780 and for Hingham, Great Ringstead, Winfarthing and the Shotesham parishes the following year. Old Buckenham and the Terrington parishes were enclosed in

1790, but the two following years are blank. On the eve of the French wars, a mere forty-one acts had been passed covering forty-eight villages and their lands. Even the six years of the war brought only another seventeen acts covering twenty-eight villages. Of the natural regions of the county only the marshland in the far west was fully enclosed before the first onslaught of acts. Eight enclosure acts were passed for Norfolk parishes in 1799, thirteen in 1800, eighteen in 1801 and nine in 1802, but the Peace of Amiens brought a lull. Only for Aslacton and for Whitwell and Hackford were acts passed in 1803. Topcroft and Denton, Crimplesham, Sporle, Bridgham, Weybourne and the town of Thetford have acts dating to 1804 but in the following six years the total for any one year was never more than double that of 1804. Only at the end of the Napoleonic Wars did the total consistently reach double figures for each year: fifteen in 1811, nineteen in 1812, eleven in 1813, twelve in 1814. But in 1815, the year of Waterloo, there are only the acts for Langham, Hindringham, Runcton Holme, Necton, Thompson and that jointly for Stoke Ferry, Wretton, Wereham and Winnold. For Larling there was an enclosure act in 1816, for Emneth and for Norton Subcourse and Heckingham acts were passed in 1817. The drive for enclosure had virtually passed. By 1821, 250 acts had been given the royal assent. The last of these years were for several parishes in a single act. In 1819, Great Melton was alone but the two others were combinations of parishes: the first for Erpingham, Colby, Banningham and Ingworth, the second covered Itteringham, Oulton, Wickmere and Wood Dalling. In 1820, Blakeney, Wiveton and Glandford were among the places granted an enclosure act and the coastal Burnhams in 1821. Between 1826 and 1867, thirty-six enclosure acts were passed concerning sixty-seven Norfolk places. Except for 1826 when four acts were passed and 1830 when three became law, only in 1829, 1840, 1841, 1849 and 1867 was there more than one act in a year. The last were for Colkirk, Tatterford and Fakenham and for Shimpling and Burston; the interaction of town and village and the farming content of the small towns survives today.

Enclosure is a hotly debated topic among historians. The final act in a gradual process is all that is recorded by an eighteenth-century or later enclosure act. Its effect in the individual village needs to be studied at village level and not subject to generalizations. Population increases are part of a general trend both in enclosed and unenclosed parishes, as Chapter VI notes of Little Dunham.

Certainly parishes which had been enclosed were able to grow more corn but the Napoleonic War demanded that a greater percentage of the land be cultivated. Rents were greater: at Shropham, enclosed in 1798, they increased from four shillings per acre to fourteen shillings and at Great Hockham, enclosed in 1795, the land had been valued at seven shillings per acre but after enclosure was let at eighteen shillings. Great increase did not always happen: at Ellingham, the old rate was fourteen or fifteen shillings per acre, but after 1798 the quality price for the best land was fifteen to seventeen shillings. The serious objection to enclosure came not from farmers who had to pay more rent but from the poor. Arthur Young's words about Ludham have a sting in the tail:

> The commons were enclosed in 1801; all cottagers that claimed had allotments; and one for fuel to the whole; but the cottages did not belong to the poor; the allotments in general went to the larger proprietors, and the poor consequently were left, in this respect destitute: many cows were kept before, few now. All the poor very much against the measure.

Poverty had that insidious effect. The commons right belonged to the landlord not the tenant and the former as at Holme Hale could be a farmer or a tradesman.

The farmers and the tradesmen were those who benefited from enclosure. The upper tradesmen were especially favoured. Eighteenth-century society was the first to require an army of professional people and they acquired some of the tastes of those whom they served. Solicitors, physicians, veterinary surgeons, masters of academies, rectors, they built the elegant, small, eighteenth-century houses in villages like Mattishall and Morston. The same late-Georgian fronts line the green of Burnham Market and that at Hingham too. They are found at Foulsham and Coltishall and at Great Massingham. The frontages are in red brick, the windows have upright sashes divided into small panes. Individual houses in the style are to be found in Ludham and Little Snoring and at Kenninghall with an extravagant porch. At Martham as at Mulbarton individual houses exude a charm lacking in many of the

Salle pulpit

Doom and screen in Ludham church

Royal arms of Elizabeth I in Ludham church

Claxton church

Shelton church, built in brick before 1489

Shipdham church, the north aisle

Great Snoring church, interior

Victorian replacement for the Saxon church at Framlingham Pigot

(*Opposite*) Mattishall, house with eighteenth-century front

Hingham, house with shaped gables of the seventeenth century

New Houghton, built 1729 onwards

Heydon, estate village of the 1790s

great houses of the period. The smaller manor houses may have it like Ditchingham Hall and Mulbarton Hall, the Georgian one where antiques are now sold.

The Georgian century was secular. Few churches were built in Norfolk villages. At Gunton there is a boring classical temple, by Robert Adam designed in 1769, which might just do justice to some craggy outcrop but it sits oddly in a sylvan glade. Nearby Thorpe Market has a more intimate structure of 1796 in nice warm red brick. There are royal arms in more than a hundred churches. Neither the late Stuarts nor the Hanoverians felt sufficiently secure to dispense with the placing of their devices in churches.

William III is represented on six sets of royal arms in Norfolk village churches. Two are dated: Bale of 1698 and two years earlier Scottow. Best known are the carved pieces at Ingworth and at Shelton; the others are those at Saxlingham Nethergate and re-lettered for George III at Morley St Botolph. Queen Anne is found in fourteen villages, including two which have been re-painted, those at Kelling (1797 for George III) and Billingford (for George II). Dated are two of 1711, at Tilney All Saints and Swanton Morley, and one of 1714, Caistor St Edmund. Earlier is the set at Fersfield, erected in 1703. Other Norfolk villages with arms erected in Queen Anne's reign (1702–14) are Redenhall, Saxthorpe, Bodham, Garboldisham, Heydon and Horstead. The board at Thompson is repainted from an earlier achievement; that at Langham is dated 1742 but has Queen Anne's device.

Comparatively speaking, few of the remaining 133 arms belong to the reign of George I. Dated to 1721 are those at Great Ellingham and at Bexwell, but those at Great Walsingham, Tibenham, Sprowston, Roydon, Halvergate, and Claxton lack an inscription giving their date. George II was on the throne for rather longer than his father, 1727 until 1760, compared with the thirteen years from 1714 to 1727. The arms at Wickhampton date to 1737, those at Castle Acre to 1748. Later in date are the arms at Brisley (1755) and Narborough (1759). Three of the thirty-two villages with achievements definitely to be ascribed to George III are dated to early years of the reign: Tottenhill (1763), Elsing (1794) and Walpole St Peter (1801). Of the period without the French designation, there is one dated example: Blakeney (1818). None of those set up during the reign of George IV is dated but for his brother, William IV, the villages of Norfolk have no fewer than eight examples. The arms at Stockton and at Merton have no date. The former are dark in their background, and the board is square. The achievements belong to the first years of the reign: 1831 at Swanton Abbot, 1832 at Brancaster and 1833 at Itteringham and Shotesham. Contemporary are the two other undated pieces, at Norton Subcourse and at Old Hunstanton. There are even examples belonging to the reign of Queen Victoria. Dated are those of 1860 at Rockland All Saints and of 1872 at Sculthorpe; undated those at East Bradenham, Great Hockham, Stradsett, Upwell and Wolferton. The device of Victoria is on one board at Denton; the achievement of her grandfather, George III, on another.

The Georgian century had a taste for minor pieces of sculpture such as funerary monuments, but enthusiasm for lavish provision for the dead declined with the restoration of Charles II. Cromwellian severity had killed it off. The black stones on the floor of Shipdham church are typical of all that the gentry could afford or their heirs wished to provide. Sarah Hare's wax effigy at Stow Bardolph seems unreal or a joke: it wears her clothes, as her will directs. The door can be opened and the figure confronts one. Her father's monument reflects the taste for the classical. More intimate are the headstones of Norfolk churchyards. Real people, if not yet village labourers, are among those remembered in more than a line in the parish register. Early gravestones are to be found at Kenninghall, Cley, Blakeney and Wheatacre to name but four churchyards. Most have a Victorian beginning like Great Dunham and Winterton, Ludham and Castle Acre. This too is a world that Parson Woodforde would have understood.

His world is not far away from the houses which line the square at Mattishall. Neither is that wherein Norfolk's most famous son, Horatio Nelson, grew up much absent from Burnham Market. Burnham Thorpe lacks now the rectory of his birth but the county showed its due in 1817 when the commemorative pillar was erected facing towards the county, not the sea, on the South Denes at Yarmouth. Trafalgar Day, 21st October 1805, is a little more important than Waterloo and certainly more English than May Day. In memory of a real hero perhaps it ought henceforth to be made a national holiday.

In the nineteenth century, the coaches were named after the

victor of Trafalgar, the *Lord Nelson* from Lynn, the various enterprises which went from Fakenham and Holt to London had names like the *Hero*, the *Nelson* and the *Patriot* and no one had any doubt as to who was meant. One splendidly named enterprise began in Wells; it was the *Norfolk Hero*. The village public house was often renamed. One on the Market Place at Burnham Market is called The Lord Nelson; there are others of the same name in Yaxham, East Bradenham, Reedham, Fakenham and at North Walsham where he had been a pupil at Paston's Grammar School. In Burnham Overy Staithe, the pub was renamed The Hero Inn, and the signboard leaves no doubt as to who is meant. In Burnham Thorpe the village pub is now The Lord Nelson. Perhaps because they are so remote, the Burnhams have never become commercialized as the Nelson centre. One can still walk across the green of Burnham Market or sail a boat from Overy Staithe and feel no pressures of the twentieth-century ugliness which so often goes with the birthplace of a great man. One can also walk along the shore of Norton Marsh or take a skiff to Scolt Head and remember that a man once did the same and wrote long letters to the Admiralty asking for the merest frigate to command as they let him rot for a decade. Nelson had the tactical genius to break the rules of ship fighting, change them for all time and win. Cape Trafalgar followed the equally illustrious victories of Copenhagen and the Nile.

VI

The Village at its Height

IN the *General View of the Agriculture of the County of Norfolk*, Arthur Young devoted just over a hundred pages to collecting some extremely detailed information about the effects of enclosure on some eighty-two Norfolk villages. Much of this concerns the increase in population both before and after the enclosure act and subsequent award of a given village. Little Dunham, in the northern part of Breckland, has two estimates of the numbers before enclosure: 172 souls in 1763, 206 people in 1792. A survey of the latter year, predating the enclosure act by two years, noted 44 families, living in 41 houses. Thirty-nine married couples had 89 children, 45 boys and 44 girls. There were rather more women than men in the village: 62 as against 55. In 1841, Little Dunham had a population of 298; in 1971 there were 192 people living there, an increase of 10 in the previous decade. Other villages where a survey was made in the eighteenth century were Oxborough and Foulden in 1782, and Ketteringham in 1787. Only 9 of the 35 houses at Oxborough were liable to window tax.

West of King's Lynn are the marshland villages: the two Terringtons, the three Tilneys, the two Walpoles, the four Wiggenhalls, West Walton and Walsoken. A populous area both in the eighteenth century and in the twentieth, like the rest of Norfolk the villages experienced their greatest increases in population in the first forty years of the nineteenth century. At Terrington St Clement there were 824 people in 1801, and 1,675 in 1841; Tilney St Lawrence grew from 362 to 762 in the same period; the increase at West Walton was no less spectacular, 513 in 1801 but 954 forty years later. Even more considerable was the growth in numbers at Walpole St Andrew. Here 227 people lived in 1801 and 565 in 1841. Neighbouring Walpole St Peter housed no fewer than 1,335 inhabitants in 1841. A survey taken of both parishes combined, Walpole St Peter and St Andrew, in 1770 maintained an enumeration of 538 souls. The survey aptly demonstrated the area. Farmers and their wives and children numbered 275, but labourers and their families only 81. There were 22 paupers maintained by the parish and 160 servants, including presumably unmarried labourers. They lived in 120 houses and all except 17 householders were occupiers of land to a greater or lesser degree. On the land, two hundred cows and three hundred horses were grazed. The numbers seem small in comparison with the ten thousand sheep.

For the last quarter of the eighteenth century the information in depth about individual Norfolk villages is partial. It can be as thin as a register of baptismal and burial numbers culled from the parish register for the final twenty years, given as summaries for the two decades as for South Walsham, Thornage and Wood Rising. All this demonstrates is the natural increase in the population, but this does not take into account the considerable migration between villages and into selected villages. On occasion there is a little more data. For Titchwell on the north Norfolk coast, the effect of enclosure following the act of 1786 was noted by Arthur Young: sheep more than doubled, meat cattle more than trebled, and corn greatly increased. Great Hockham was enclosed in 1795, less than a decade before Young published his collection of findings in 1804. Much of the corn arable land was left in grass for sheep-walk, perhaps half of the 1,293 hectares (3,196 acres) of the parish, but the rest gave greatly increased yields of corn. If the cows at Great Hockham had neither increased nor much decreased, the sheep were increased.

Sheep and men increased in the early nineteenth century; men decreased thereafter. Just at the time when the population was at its greatest, the 1840s and the 1850s, commercial directories began to appear in great numbers. There are earlier almanacs, and the earliest directories tend to be confined to the towns. The first to cover Norfolk was issued by a Manchester firm headed by a man named Pigot in 1822. Further issues of his directory were made for Norfolk in 1830 and in 1839, while his successor, Slater, issued directories in 1850 and in 1852. Norfolk was invariably part of a much larger group of counties. In 1822, the villages were totally omitted; the towns were the three largest, Norwich, Great Yarmouth and King's Lynn, and the more obvious of those with a thousand to three thousand people: Attleborough, Aylsham, Cromer, Diss, Downham Market, Fakenham, Holt, North Walsham, Swaffham, Thetford, Great Walsingham and Wells. East Dereham and Wymondham were larger than the rest. Included also were Burnham Market, Cley-next-the-Sea and Watton, all under a thousand people, and Hingham which by 1841 boasted 1,691 people. The 1839 edition covered more places: Briston, Old and New Buckenham, Cawston, Coltishall, North Elmham, Foulsham, Harleston, East Harling, Kenninghall, Letheringsett, Loddon, Reepham, Scole, Shipdham, Swanton Abbot, Swanton Morley and Worstead. Most of these were then, as now, villages rather than towns.

In contrast to the publications of Pigot and of Slater, the Sheffield firm of William White attempted in the *History, Gazetteer and Directory of Norfolk, and the city and county of the city of Norwich* to cover each locality in the county; this volume went through six separate editions. The first of 1836 is rare, the second of 1845 readily available through a reprint of 1969; later editions are those of 1854, 1864, 1883 and 1890. Contemporary with these are the various issues of *Kelly's Directory* which appeared in 1846 with a directory for Suffolk and Cambridgeshire. Further issues were made in 1853 and 1858; after 1865 the interval between editions is four year, occasionally longer, to the last issue in 1937. For the mid-nineteenth century one other firm is valuable. E. Hunt and Co. brought out a *Directory of East Norfolk with part of Suffolk* in 1850. It includes parishes as far west as Great Fransham, Little Fransham, Little Dunham, Beeston, Litcham and Mileham. To the north-east of these, North Elmham, Guist, Foulsham, Reepham, Cawston, Oulton, Aylsham, Blickling, and Erpingham form the boundary of the area covered. Villages noted north of this are Trunch, Knapton, Northrepps, Southrepps and Mundesley; Gimingham, Trimingham, Sidestrand and Overstrand are not included, although Cromer is. South of Norwich, from the London road north the bounds are Attleborough, Great Ellingham, Hingham, Wood Rising, Cranworth and Shipdham. South of the London road, Old Buckenham, Banham, Kenninghall, East Harling and the Lophams are the boundary of the directory's coverage; Garboldisham and Blo' Norton are omitted. The area is instructive. Including also the villages of Lothingland (then wholely in Suffolk) and the southern bank of the River Waveney, chiefly Beccles and Bungay, the compiler unconsciously gave expression to a Norwich man's view of Norfolk. It is still the area easily accessible by public transport from the county capital. Hunt included 160 villages, William White noted the principal inhabitants, commercial, agricultural and other statistical information about all eight hundred of the county's villages.

Oxborough and Foulden have already been mentioned in this chapter. At Oxborough, the great gatehouse of Oxburgh Hall attracts attention; the parish church of St John the Evangelist is a shell of itself: the spire rising 47·58 metres (156 feet) fell in 1948. Here Bedingfelds were buried in almost regal state for two hundred years from the beginning of the sixteenth century to 1704. These were Catholic gentry and they remained adherents of the old faith through to the happier times of Victorian England. In 1835, Sir Henry Richard Paston Bedingfeld built a chapel adjacent to the great gatehouse. He was buried there in 1862; a tomb lavish in its conception bearing a recumbent effigy in white marble commemorates the man who did much to rehabilitate his ancestral home. He rebuilt the house from 1835 onwards, razing the reconstruction of 1778. His chaplain was of his own creed: the Rev. William Gubbins in 1845; but doubtless he and the lord of the manor lived in amity with the Rev. Richard Lucas, M.A., Rector of Oxborough and Vicar of Foulden. At the latter a curate, the Rev. J. H. Clubbe, resided as perhaps befitted a separate village with its own hall. William George Tyssen Daniel Tyssen resided at what William White in 1845 called a "modern mansion" although its core and some of the chimneys suggest a house originally put up a hundred years or so after Oxburgh Hall. Tyssen was High Sheriff of Norfolk in 1843: the office still carried prestige and if not exactly sought after was not unwelcome to those who wished to be seen to be taking an active part in county ceremonies.

The social context of the mid-nineteenth century may be read in William White's directory for 1845. William Ford, butler at the hall, was among those noted as tradespeople at Foulden. At Oxborough, no such servants were recorded: they were clearly too lowly to warrant recognition, like the mass of labourers who formed the majority of the village population here as elsewhere in Norfolk. A schoolmaster, a blacksmith, 4 farmers, a grocer and draper, with Thomas Roan who kept the Spread Eagle, were those of middling importance at Oxborough. Foulden, being larger, could boast a slightly wider range of trades: a smith and farrier as well as a blacksmith, Robert Dorman at the Bell was also a wheelwright but William Hardy at the Chequers had no other trade. Two beerhouses were noted, one of which was also a shop, and one of the 6 farmers was noted as being also a shopkeeper. Another, John Carter, was also a carpenter. None of the farmers in either Foulden or Oxborough are noted as owning the land they tilled; at Gooderstone (the village between them, north of Foulden), 4 of the 9 farmers were owners. Gooderstone was noted as a milling village. Charles Brooke and Mallows Garrod were corn millers with two windmills and a watermill; James Brook worked a third windmill in the parish. Other tradesmen in the village were 2 shoemakers, a butcher, a shopkeeper, a blacksmith and a wheelwright.

The horse trades served both the farming community and the residents of the big house. Often the hall would have horse servants among its staff. The early Victorian years were the high noon of country house society and villages based on the big house, also called "the hall". In the villages between the River Wissey and the River Nar and east of the River Great Ouse, the big house was common. Apart from Oxburgh Hall and Foulden Hall, there was Henry Berney Caldwell at Hillborough Hall, Edward Thornhill Applewhaite at South Pickenham Hall, Theophilus Russell Buckworth at Cockley-Cley Hall, William Maybohm Rider Haggard at West Bradenham Hall, and Andrew Fountaine at Narford Hall, together with Samuel Tyssen who was occasionally resident at his seat, Narborough Hall. West of South Greenhoe Hundred, Clackclose Hundred was equally gentry country: Ryston Hall, Stow Bardolph Hall and Stradsett Hall were respectively the seats of Edward Roger Pratt, Sir Thomas Hare, Baronet, and William Bragge, M.P., while Mrs Allen resided at Shouldham Hall. Fincham Hall, however, was used as a farmhouse.

The area contained some villages which could hardly be classed as other than a few houses: Stradsett was described as "a few scattered houses near the Swaffham road", Shingham had only 59 souls and about a thousand acres of land "all in one farm". Robert Gilling and Henry Norbourn occupied the two farms in Roxham, now Roxham Farm and Crossways Farm. The former village is now amalgamated with Ryston, but this in 1845 was only 40 people, the occupants and employees of the Hall. Bexwell was "seventy inhabitants, three houses, six cottages and 1,104 acres". Bodney was "only one house and a few scattered cottages"; Houghton-on-the-Hill was occupied by non-residents and except for the farm steward who lived in the largest house, there were only the residents of five cottages. Away from here in Shropham Hundred, the entry for Illington is equally poignant:

> Illington . . . comprises only ninety-three inhabitants and eleven hundred acres of land, all the property of the Rev Robert Churchman Long, the lord of the manor and patron and incumbent of the rectory. Francis Hamond Gates *farms the parish.*

Kilverstone was another parish of which it was said: "besides the Hall there are only a few cottages." These are villages which have not survived into the twentieth century.

Much of the remaining hundreds of the area which in 1974 became the West Norfolk District was already sharply divided between the thriving and the decayed villages. In Smithdon Hundred, Barwick, Bircham Newton, Bircham Tofts, Fring, Shernbourne and Titchwell were all miniscule; Choseley was an extra-parochial farm occupied by Thomas Rodwell and Barret-Ringstead comprised a decayed parish now only one farm occupied by Martin Dodman. In contrast other villages were thriving. Docking had increased in population from 777 in 1801 to 1,537 in 1841. Its range of services was wider than any noticed hitherto. There were 9 farmers, 8 shoemakers, one of whom was also a hosier, 5 joiners including Thomas Clark who is described as "joiner and wheelwright", 4 tailors, 4 grocers and drapers and 3 blacksmiths. There were two each of such diverse trades as farrier, baker, miller and baker, and dressmaker, and one each of miller and butcher, tinner and brazier, confectioner, straw-hat maker, coal dealer, cabinet maker, druggist, music master, bricklayer, tea dealer, cooper and basket maker. There were 3 surgeons, and also 3 men described as plumber, painter, etc. There was also the workhouse of Docking Union, built in 1836 to the designs of John Brown; it is now Burnstack. Further along the road to Heacham is Sedgeford, only 669 people in 1841, a contrast with its neighbour. There were 12 farmers, 3 shoemakers, 3 grocers and drapers and 2 blacksmiths. The carpenter was also the parish clerk and the bricklayer kept a beerhouse. There was another beer seller and 2 victuallers at The Buck and The King's Head. A father and son were tailors and there was also a schoolmaster, a baker and a basket maker. Heacham had been a town; a great fire destroyed the market in the early seventeenth century. It was a growing parish; between 1801 and 1841 the population grew from 524 to 821 and if not as well provided as Docking the range of tradespeople was considerable. There were 15 farmers, and 4 each of those described as beerhouse keeper, grocer and draper, and shoemaker. Benjamin, Francis and George Bly were respectively a wheelwright, a carpenter and a plumber and painter; the two last had no competition but there was another wheelwright in 1845 as well as a joiner, a blacksmith, a tinner, 2 butchers and a miller and baker. Another miller maintained premises both at Heacham and at Ringstead to the north-east. Clergy were well represented at Heacham: the vicar, who was also among the chief landowners, the curate and the curate of Snettisham all lived there; Snettisham had, too, its own resident vicar.

Away from the coast this is a barren area, in the late twentieth century rapidly becoming depopulated. Great Bircham was not a large village in 1845 but it could boast 3 grocers, 2 blacksmiths, a wheelwright, a joiner, a tailor, a corn miller, a machine maker and a shoemaker who had the delightful name of Thomas Shildrake, as well as 4 farmers in the population of 511. Bircham Tofts and Bircham Newton were separate then; both were farming communities with populations respectively of 107 and 142 in 1841. The windmill is now derelict, and the church of Bircham Tofts lacks a roof and all vestiges of a chancel. The best has survived of the flint farms and the flint cottages, part of the estate of the Marquis of Cholmondeley: Houghton Park is immediately to the south.

Away to the north-east is a unique group of parishes, the Burnhams. There are seven Burnhams; three, Burnham Westgate, Burnham Sutton and Burnham Ulph form the small market town of Burnham Market, or at least in 1845 it so remained. Today it is more a large village and so merits inclusion in this book. These three are close to one another; Burnham Norton and Burnham Overy begin less than a mile away. Only the two on the coast are distant: Burnham Deepdale to the west, Overy Staithe to the east. Burnham Thorpe, of Nelson fame, is tucked away in folds of the hills on the other side of the River Burn. In 1845, the Burnhams illustrated the difference between village and town. A joiner, a blacksmith, a wheelwright and beer seller, 2 farmers and a coal dealer were the tradesmen of Burnham Norton; the curate lived at Brancaster beyond Burnham Deepdale. Both Burnham Overy and Burnham Thorpe were more populous: 613 and 396 inhabitants respectively in 1841. At Overy Staithe, there were corn, coal and coke merchants, a master mariner, and a miller and maltster but the farmers were recorded as living in Burnham Overy. At Burnham Thorpe, apart from 6 farmers there was a schoolmaster, a parish clerk, a shopkeeper, a bricklayer, a baker and grocer, a blacksmith and a wheelwright, James Brett, who also kept the local public house, not surprisingly named The Nelson. Yet at Burnham Market, despite its already declining status as a market town there were men who would not be found in a village: 2 solicitors, a stationer, an engraver, an organ builder, a hairdresser, an ironmonger, and 2 academies which took boarders. The usual range of rural town trades was present: bricklayer, mason, brazier, saddler, plumber and painter, baker, blacksmith, shoemaker, butcher, joiner and tailor. From Burnham Market a sociable (a horse-drawn omnibus) ran to King's Lynn and Wells on Mondays, Wednesdays and Fridays; its own small market for provisions was held on a Saturday.

In most of the places noted, at least among the larger villages, there was already a school but Burnham Market alone had a subscription library. An interesting contrast of village and town in the early Victorian years comes from opposite ends of Norfolk. Walpole St Peter and Harleston were about the same size. In 1841 their populations were 1,355 and 1,425 respectively. At the former there was a brewer, a saddler, a schoolmaster, a tailor, a veterinary surgeon, a plumber and an auctioneer. There were 5 public houses and 5 beerhouses; 3 shoemakers, 3 shopkeepers, 3 wheelwrights, 4 blacksmiths, 2 butchers, 2 millers and 43 farmers completed the catalogue of the principal inhabitants of Walpole St Peter. The difference from Harleston is considerable. In the town there was a gasworks, erected in 1840, a farmers' club, a savings bank, a Free School, and schools run by both the two early nineteenth-century promotional societies. There were far more tradesmen; the range was greater. There was more than one attorney, auctioneer, bookseller, brazier and tinman, cabinet maker, chemist, coach builder (or better class of wheelwright), confectioner, cooper, currier, grocer, hairdresser, ironmonger, joiner, miller, plumber, glazier and painter, saddler, straw-hat maker, surgeon, tailor, watchmaker, and wine, spirit, ale and porter merchant. Seven insurance companies maintained some form of agency and there were two banks other than the savings bank. One of the banks, the East of England, maintained a branch; the other, Gurneys, Turner and Brightwen, used a solicitor as their agent. William Hazard was also the magistrates' clerk; for convivial discourse he had a range of gentlemen on whom he might call, plus several persons of independent means. The atmosphere was altogether different from a mere village, even one as populous as Walpole St Peter.

There were, of course, farmers; no small town in early Victorian England was without its husbandmen. In 1845, William White noted 19 at Harleston, a total which included those whose land was at Redenhall. In 1789 the population had been 1,344 for Harleston and Redenhall; they formed 231 households. Of these 38 were husbandmen, 26 were spinners, 15 were shoemakers and 8 were carpenters. Twelve were farmers, and 10 families were dependent for their income on the town's brewery. There were 12 publicans. A range of trades each supported a single household: painter, chaise-driver, gardener, whitesmith, hosier, mason, knitter, heelmaker, brickmaker, sawyer, brazier, gelder, midwife, nurse, milkwoman, ironer, bookseller, milliner, molecatcher, wheelwright and rector. The last, naturally, considered himself the social equal of the 5 gentlemen and gentlewomen, and somewhat the social superior of the 5 schoolmasters and mistresses. There were 5 butchers and 5 blacksmiths, but again the range was considerable for the trades with two representatives in Harleston in 1789: millwright, fruiterer, draper, cooper, china and earthenware dealer, ostler, breeches-maker, drover and woolcomber. Three each were saddlers, attorneys, surgeons, barbers and thatchers; there were 4 grocers, 6 bakers, 6 weavers, and 8 tailors. Although no one is listed in 1845 as keeping a servants' registry office, there were no fewer than 185 servants in Harleston in 1789. The males of these and the farm labourers formed a sizeable percentage of the younger element among those noted aged between fifteen and sixty in 1798. The militia return of that year showed that 27 were incapable of active service through some infirmity such as being lame or deaf or maimed. If Walpole in 1770 was massively more sheep than men, at Harleston in 1798 the full total of beasts was less than the human beings. Animals numbered 1,371, inhabitants 1,464. Pigs and sheep were the most numerous beasts: 414 and 475 respectively; there were 119 cows, 63 oxen (including ploughing beasts), and 129 young cattle. Horses, a subject of vital importance to the government, were divided into riding horses (32) and cart horses (139). In the rural town, the emphasis was very much on the world of work.

Work, not leisure, and certainly not pleasure, dominated people's lives in the Norfolk village in the early and middle years of the nineteenth century. William White is never the full story. A directory is concerned to paint a favourable picture of the area. The poverty is conveniently brushed aside; the degradation of harsh unremitting toil is what those who became articulate later in the century remembered. The first accounts by ordinary villagers are later; they recall a world similar to and coeval with that recorded by William White's correspondents.

Symbol of the poverty of those whom the later Victorians were pleased to call the multitude was the workhouse. To the Norfolk village this was not a total innovation in 1834 when the Poor Law Amendment Act was passed. A workhouse had been built at Heckingham in 1763 and one at Gressenhall in 1776. Three were built in 1805, at Coltishall, Gimingham and Sheringham. However, some were new in the 1830s: Swainsthorpe, Great Snoring, Rockland All Saints and Kenninghall were all parishes where the new edifice was erected. The workhouse for Forehoe Union was typical. Built in 1776, it had accommodation for four hundred. In July 1841 there were 135 inmates; six more resided there in November 1844.

The fear of the workhouse was terrible enough. George Edwards was born at Marsham, on 5th October 1850. The household was poor and life had a poverty the twentieth century finds hard to envisage let alone to comprehend. Food for his mother was onion gruel, for the new-born infant skimmed milk soaked into bread. His father, a bullock feeder, earned eight shillings a week, from which he was expected to feed and clothe himself and his wife and their six children as well as pay the rent on their two-roomed cottage. The pay had been nine shillings but with the repeal of the Corn Laws in 1846 a shilling a week was deducted from the sum paid to labourers. The wages did not buy much: a four-pound loaf cost a shilling, an ounce of tea was charged at sixpence and a pound of sugar at eightpence. Cheese, a vital source of protein, for meat was rarely if ever eaten, cost sevenpence a pound before the Crimean War, one shilling and sixpence after it had been started. War had always been a motor of inflation. Children as young as ten worked in the fields for the pittance of a shilling and twopence a week; at twelve the pay was the more princely sum of a shilling and sixpence. Children even younger than this were put to work at as early a date as possible: George Edwards was six when he started work scaring crows in the fields for a shilling a week. He worked each of the seven days for this.

By then Europe had experienced the terrible winter of 1854–5 and George Edwards himself had been an inmate of the workhouse at Buxton. To help feed his starving family, his father had lifted a handful of turnips from the field he cultivated for the farmer for whom he worked. One night the farm labourer was apprehended; the magistrates the next morning committed him to prison for fourteen days' hard labour; the family were taken to the workhouse, there was nowhere else for them to go. They stayed there all through the winter; there was no work for a man whom society "branded as a thief" because George Edwards later wrote, "a nation that would not allow his father sufficient income to feed his children was responsible for any breach of the law he might have committed."

In the spring of 1856, George Edwards' father took his family out of the workhouse and back to Marsham; he had obtained work at Alby making bricks. Marsham is three kilometres (two miles) south of Aylsham; Alby is eight kilometres (five miles) north of the town. Away all week, he made bricks at four shillings per thousand. The father and another of his sons took home thirteen shillings each week. Brickmaking was a trade of increasing importance in early Victorian Norfolk. It was largely a village trade. Of the villages in Hunt's *Directory* in 1850, ten villages had a brickmaker among their tradespeople. At Morningthorpe, Alfred Goldsmith combined cider making and brickmaking; John and Jonathan Hunt at Banham were joiners and brickmakers, but George Gilbert was a brickmaker only. These, of course, were the master men, not the journeymen. A family as lowly in its social status as that of George Edwards' parents would not have figured in the view of a directory compiler.

A village famed for its brickmakers was Reedham; the riverine clay was especially suitable for brickmaking. The village inn was called the Brickmakers' Arms. An early Victorian photographer recorded the brickfields with their horse gin. A horse walked round and round a central drum puddling the clay, improving its viscosity, and making the material more easy to work. Bricks were made by hand. George Edwards' father at Alby had to turn the clay three times before pressing the raw material into a mould. Cold bricks were left to dry and set before being fired in clamp kilns. Often these were near woods. The bricks for the mid-Victorian Bylaugh Hall were made at Kerdiston, north of Reepham, where there is a Brick Kiln Farm which has a small wood attached. There is a Brick Kiln Plantation at Beechamwell and a Brickkiln Farm within the woods north-east of Wilton.

Brickmaking because of the raw material is more obviously a village trade, but another Victorian photograph of Reedham shows the brewery. Because of the brewery, the village had a cooper in 1845: it is not listed by Hunt. The village cooper in the early Victorian years is perhaps a poor example of an occupation one would not readily envisage as a village trade. Other villages with a cooper in 1850 were Martham and Mattishall. Both, with over a thousand people, are ideal examples of the early Victorian village. Hunt described Mattishall as

> a large village, once deriving considerable importance from its manufactures, but now entirely dependent on agriculture for support. Malting and corn-grinding furnish employment for some of its inhabitants and farming operations require the assistance of many others.

Farming in the early Victorian years was largely unmechanized and jobs such as sowing and harvesting, let alone weeding, required hands by the score. Above the labouring population there was a stratum of village skill: some recognized as individual trades, some less easily quantified. Baker, butcher, blacksmith, carpenter, corn miller, grocer, plumber and painter, saddler, shoemaker and wheelwright are common to many if not all large villages, as too, probably, are a farrier, a veterinary surgeon and a tailor. Both Martham and Mattishall could boast a watchmaker in 1845; both also had a surgeon in 1850. Less usual were the basket maker at Martham in 1845 and the cabinet maker at Mattishall. A resident surgeon, which both villages had, was not usual. However, a resident clergyman was. At Martham, there was a curate also, both in 1845 and in 1850. Of the 166 villages listed by Hunt in 1850, no fewer than twenty had a curate in addition to the incumbent. Reepham had three Anglican clergymen resident there, but the Venerable John B. Collyer, M.A., of Hackford Hall was Archdeacon of Norwich. Thomas Chute Ellis Warcup, the curate, was also a graduate; the patron and incumbent of Reepham Parish Church, the Rev. Frederick Field, was not. Early Victorian clergy, especially those aged under forty, tended to have had a university education. The same was to become true of the children of the principal landowners, as Bateman's *Directory of Landowners* of 1873 makes clear.

South Walsham was a village which in 1845 and in 1850 could boast both an incumbent and a curate. The Rev. John Toplis, B.D., was the incumbent in both years, but the Rev. Henry Joseph Muskett, B.A., curate in 1845, had moved away; his place was taken by the Rev. Thomas Wren. South Walsham retained two churches almost to the Victorian age, but on 30th June 1827 a fire destroyed the roof and interior of St Lawrence's Church; the chancel was repaired and re-opened in 1832, the tower left a ruin, the nave destroyed. Also destroyed in the fire were four barns of William Jary, the vicarage barns, three wheat stacks, a hay stack, a dwelling house and some other property. Hot ashes had been thrown on dry manure; the conflagration was spectacular but not untypical of the hazards of village life in the early nineteenth century. Insurance, however, had penetrated into village life. At New Buckenham, George Hall was a broker and agent to the Norwich Union and Hail Storm Insurance Companies.

New Buckenham was also a village without a resident clergyman. William Fison was the incumbent and seems not to have kept a curate. Forty villages of those listed by Hunt were similarly without resident clergy. Some like Beeston St Lawrence, Whitlingham and Little Ormesby had less than a hundred inhabitants. Others were consolidated benefices: Kimberley with Barnham Broom, but this in 1850 supported both a rector and a curate; at others the rector lived out of the parish. The Rev. John

Burroughes, who held the livings of Burlingham St Andrew and St Peter consolidated with Burlingham St Edmund, lived at Lingwood. Livings were being amalgamated. Great Ellingham vicarage and Little Ellingham rectory had been jointly held since the early eighteenth century. Tivetshall St Mary and Tivetshall St Margaret were held by J. N. White in 1845 and by F. S. Bignold in 1850. Great Fransham and Little Fransham, however, maintained a resident rector each and neither village was large; the first 329 in 1841, the second 263.

By the early Victorian years, the Anglicans were not the only resident clergy in the Norfolk village. More villages had chapels than resident ministers. However, in 1850, there were Baptist ministers at Brooke, Catton, Costessey, Great Ellingham, Ingham, and Kenninghall. The Baptist minister at Forncett St Peter also maintained a school and there were independent ministers at Mattishall and Denton. Wortwell had both an independent and a Baptist minister. There was a Roman Catholic priest at Costessey. Chapels were found in many villages. In Launditch Hundred, many of the villages were served only by the parish church, yet Great Dunham, with only 520 people, had small chapels for the Baptists, the Wesleyan Methodists and the Primitive Methodists; both Methodist sects had chapels at Litcham and there was a Baptist chapel at North Elmham in 1845. The relative newness of Methodism is shown by the dates of the building of chapels at Caister-on-Sea: Wesleyan in 1820, Primitive in 1837. Elsewhere in East Flegg Hundred, Filby had Methodist and Unitarian chapels and there were two Methodist chapels in Stokesby-cum-Heringby. Martham was not the only parish of which it was said, "The Baptists, and the Wesleyan and Primitive Methodists, have each a chapel here."

One of the most delightful early chapels is that built for the Particular Baptists in Kenninghall. The congregation was formed in 1799 under the ministry of the Rev. Thomas Smith of Shelfanger. Henry Howell was the pastor in 1845.

In 1845, William White captured a world before the great change of the nineteenth century: railways. There was one line in Norfolk open when he made the compilation in November 1844. The line from Norwich to Yarmouth via Brundall and Reedham with stations also at Buckenham and Cantley had been opened on 1st May 1844. By 1850 a new element had arisen in village occupations. Both Great Fransham and Bradstone had men whose trade was described as railway clerk. Yet for more than half a century beyond, agriculture and its attendant crafts would be dominant in the life of the Norfolk village.

VII

Villages and the Railway

ALMOST as the villages of Norfolk reached their most populous heights, change came. In some, decline was already beginning when the first railway in the county was opened on 30th April 1844. Running from Norwich to Yarmouth, it affected no village east of Reedham; even today the fastest part of the journey is across the wastes of Reedham Marshes, Beighton Marshes, Halvergate Marshes and Acle Marshes. West of the large village of Reedham, where the population was noted as being 614 persons in 1841, the railway affected the parishes of Blofield Hundred, along the northern bank of the River Yare. Stations were built at Cantley, Buckenham Ferry, Brundall and originally at Brandon Junction, where the line between Brandon and Norwich, via Thetford and Wymondham, met the first Norfolk railway. The railway to Brandon, which joined Norwich to London, was opened in July 1845. If this introduction has concentrated too much on towns, it may be forgiven; early railways in Norfolk were designed to connect towns, not to serve villages. Indeed as any regular traveller between Cambridge and Norwich is only too painfully aware, the railway has few stations in Norfolk. Those extant, which is all except one of the six originally provided, are served now by pay-trains but their names reveal their remoteness. Eccles Road and Harling Road are each distant from the villages to which they refer. It is three kilometres (two miles) from Harling Road Station to East Harling village. Similarly, the now closed station for Hethersett is over a kilometre from the main road and a further two kilometres from the village. Spooner Row, where by no means all of the trains call, alone seems close to the place which gives the station a name. The station, in 1978, slowly being demolished to leave only the platforms, may be the cause of new building in what is otherwise a remote area.

The first two railways in Norfolk, then, were designed to link towns: Norwich to Yarmouth and Norwich to Ely, Cambridge and London. Another railway from Norwich to London was opened in 1846, using the route via Ipswich. A string of Norfolk villages along the line had stations: Swainsthorpe, Flordon, Forncett, Tivetshall and Burston. Swainsthorpe, now a remnant of the north-bound platform and a kerb of the other, is close to the village but Tivetshall and Burston were both far from their respective villages. Tivetshall was in the north-west corner of Tivetshall St Margaret parish, a good two kilometres (one-and-a-half miles) from the village of Tivetshall St Mary, and with no really direct road from the village centres. Even on this line there were many villages without a station: Caistor St Edmund, Stoke Holy Cross, Newton Flotman, Tharston, Moulton St Michael and Gissing. Tasburgh, Scole and Long Stratton on the old coaching road were completely bypassed. Scole, in particular, had good cause not to love the railway; the trains took away the livelihood of many of its inhabitants. In 1845 the village was populous: four years earlier the census noted 685 inhabitants. In Diss Hundred, excluding the town which gave the ancient administrative division its name, only Winfarthing, Dickleburgh and Bressingham were comparable in numbers. Scole Inn was one of the most famed inns of the country. Here stage coaches changed horses, the first change out from Norwich. With an Easter Tuesday fair for horses, it is perhaps small wonder that among the tradesmen was George Hill, horse dealer, and while many villages had blacksmith and wheelwright, their services were much in demand in this place.

A railway was built from the Norwich to Yarmouth line at Reedham to connect Lowestoft with Norwich. A swing bridge still takes the track across the River Yare and along the New Cut, a scheme sanctioned in 1827 and completed in 1833 whereby seagoing vessels could reach Norwich. Canal and railway take the same straight course across Thurlton Marshes and those of Thorpe and Haddiscoe. On the marshes a station was built for Haddiscoe, not quite where the modern halt is. There are slight traces of the first station where the old turnpike road crossed the former bridge into St Olaves: a vast cantilevered road rides high above railway and river a good way north of Haddiscoe village. There a toll gate stood until twenty years after the railway came. When the road was opened to traffic free from impost, a pillar was erected. The west (road) face reads:

Station 1½ miles
Yarmouth 9 miles
Lowestoft 15 miles
Tollgate removed 1869

Two other faces note the road distances to Beccles (6 miles), Bungay (10 miles), Loddon (6 miles) and Norwich (16 miles) on that to the south and Aldeby (1½ miles), Wheatacre and Burgh St Peter (4 miles) on the northern side: the eastern side has no inscription.

As the monument indicates, Haddiscoe station is a remote place where, shorn of all buildings and out on the marshes with only the cows for company, the waiting traveller feels alone. There can be few places on earth more desolate than Haddiscoe station at dusk, with the mist rising from the marshes, the sun setting slowly over the giant new span of the road bridge from St Olaves with power lines raised high above the seaway. As with so many Norfolk villages the railway station is not near the village.

Railways came to West Norfolk in 1846, reaching Ely in 1847, but again few villages were affected as the line was, and is, designed to connect King's Lynn with London. Denver and Hilgay have lost their stations but that at Magdalen Road, between Watlington and Wiggenhall St Mary Magdalen, was reopened for passenger traffic in 1974. Contemporary with the railway to London was the construction of a line from King's Lynn to Norwich, joining the Cambridge to Norwich line at Wymondham. The Lynn and Dereham Railway Act received the royal assent on 21st July 1845. On 27th October 1846 the single-track railway was opened from Lynn to Narborough. On 10th August 1847 trains ran into Swaffham, and on 26th October of the same year the line reached Sporle but it was not until 11th September 1848 that the line finally arrived at East Dereham. Here it joined the line from Wymondham to Fakenham, opened in 1848, and extended to Wells in 1857. Again towns rather than villages were served.

Middleton, Narborough, Little Dunham, Fransham and Wendling were the villages with stations on the Lynn and Dereham Railway. Not all stations were near the village. Middleton was close to the fifteenth-century brick house, Middleton Towers, but nearly three kilometres (two miles) from the village. The station called Dunham was in the smaller of the two settlements, Little Dunham, but two kilometres from the much larger Great Dunham. The scattered village of Great Fransham had 329 inhabitants in 1841; its neighbour, the more compact Little Fransham, housed 263 people. The station was in the northern part of the former.

The line to Wells was a double-track railway. Stations were built to serve a number of villages, but again not always very near the village centres. Kimberley station attracted a few houses near it, now designated the hamlet of Kimberley Street, but Hardingham station was two kilometres from the village. Thuxton and Yaxham both had station near the village and the parish of North Elmham had two stations. One was at the far end of the village from the church but was close to where most of the inhabitants lived, and still live. The other, in the extreme north-east corner of the parish was called County School. Great Ryburgh and Little Walsingham were both stations in the middle of the village; Wighton Halt was behind the houses of the village.

Only one other line had been opened to serve Norfolk villages when the Great Eastern Railway was formed out of the existing plethora of small, inefficient railway companies, whose reputation was for poor service and slow trains. This was a line from Tivetshall to Bungay. At Pulham Market and Pulham St Mary the station was a good ten minutes' walk from the village; the same was true of Ditchingham, Ellingham and Geldeston stations on the extension from Bungay to Beccles opened on 2nd March 1863. Thereafter the Waveney Valley Railway became part of the Great Eastern. Another of the constituents of the Great Eastern was the East Suffolk Railway. This began as the Halesworth, Beccles and Haddiscoe Railway, authorized on 5th June 1851, and opened for passengers on 4th December 1854: goods had run two weeks earlier. One Norfolk village gained a station: Aldeby. Villages of Lothingland, then in Suffolk but since 1974 in Norfolk, were also provided with stations: Fritton and Belton and Burgh Castle which was in the centre of Belton. These were opened on 1st June 1859 when the line was extended from Haddiscoe to Great Yarmouth. But this was essentially a line to speed the journey from Yarmouth to London. Local trains were provided; their twisting route has determined the way their successor, the omnibus from Yarmouth to Beccles, runs.

The Great Eastern Railway was structured to take people from Norwich, Yarmouth, King's Lynn and Thetford to London and as a subsidiary function from Norwich to Wells and from Norwich to King's Lynn. The main function is that which the lines retain in the 1970s and will presumably have in the remainder of the twentieth century. It was also a monopoly.

It absorbed the smaller bits and pieces of railway built in the two decades following its creation. A line, the East Norfolk Railway, was built to Cromer in 1877 with a branch to Aylsham. Operated by the Great Eastern from the beginning, the giant took over the infant, underfinanced and poorly sited, in 1882. Worstead station is two kilometres from the village; Salhouse station is on the border with Rackheath parish and two kilometres at least from the nearest houses; Wroxham station is actually in Hoveton.

Much of this distance and the bad siting of stations did not matter in Victorian and Edwardian England. Farmers had carts; their produce could easily be taken to the railway. Freight was a major customer of the lines: Reedham station retains a huge area excavated for the station yard. Coal came in, agricultural produce went out.

The export of foodstuffs was attractive. In the Midlands, towns arose requiring regular supplies of vegetables, bread, meat. To this market, landowners in north Norfolk cast their eyes and felt that the Great Eastern Railway had dealt them a raw deal. Railway companies too looked at Norfolk and thought the time had come to exploit the growing prospect of holiday traffic, especially after Bank Holidays were instituted in 1871, and to cater for the farm produce. However, passenger traffic from the thinly peopled villages of Norfolk was never likely to be more than sparse. The trains which people remember of the lines built in the early 1880s are those known as 'The Leicesters', fast express trains from Norwich to Leicester, via Melton Constable, Fakenham, King's Lynn and Sutton Bridge, on through south Lincolnshire to Spalding and Bourne to Little Bytham Junction. This splendidly named place had no station, it was merely where the Midland Railway from Leicester and Melton Mowbray met end-to-end with its protégé, the Midland and Great Northern Joint Railway, known as the "muddle and go nowhere" line to its critics, who were many; it also received affectionate tributes from its devotees. To the latter it was the main line from Norfolk to the Midlands but again it was a line for long-distance travellers, not for the villages.

The M.G.N.J., the convenient shorthand from its initials, began as a string of separate railways, rarely other than single track, which ultimately linked Yarmouth with South Lynn, across North Norfolk, but not following the coast. North Walsham and Fakenham were the main towns served, with between them a place the railway changed out of all recognition. In 1845, *White's Directory* described Melton Constable with Burgh Parva as

> a fertile parish of 1700 acres, south-west-by-south of Holt and east-north-east of Fakenham. They had 114 inhabitants in 1831, but only 75 in 1841, several families having emigrated to America.

The parish was clearly not one where a revival might be expected. Burgh Parva was noted as having 400 acres belonging to Lord Hastings, whose park occupies 800 acres of the 1,300 acres of Melton Constable. A mansion rebuilt in 1680 is noted and the park was described as well stocked with deer. The inhabitants worth noting were the owner, the rector, a single farmer and an auctioneer and valuer.

Yet the place was transformed in the 1880s. The Eastern and Midlands Railway was born on 1st January 1883, taking over the Yarmouth and North Norfolk (Light) Railway of 1878, and the Lynn and Fakenham Railway of 1880. Melton Constable was its junction village. The through line from Yarmouth to Lynn was joined by lines from Norwich and after 1887 to Cromer. Melton Constable today, despite the fact that no trains have been seen since 1964, and the whole of the system from Yarmouth and Norwich to Lynn and beyond was closed on 28th February 1959, looks like a miniature Derby. Indeed it was a miniature Derby, a railway village in the centre of farmland.

Derby, indeed, was very much the inspiration for this innovation in the Norfolk countryside. Serried ranks of terraced houses give the appearance of an East Midlands town, but there are just too few of them: three streets south of the main road from Melton

Constable to Briston and three to the north. The impression soon fades; the Eastern Counties omnibus takes the traveller into Briston in less than five minutes. Industrial life, however, came to this Norfolk village. In 1881, there were 118 people; in 1891, the figure had risen to 393; twenty years later no fewer than 1,157 people lived in Melton Constable. Opinions vary about the houses in Melton Constable. One, frequently expressed, complaint stresses the depressing nature of the terraces of twenty or so houses with larger dwellings at their ends. They have been described as "the ugliest in Norfolk", yet there is much in the towns, especially Great Yarmouth, of much greater oppressiveness. As a Norfolk village which *is* different, Melton Constable despite its remoteness is well worth visiting, even for the non-railway buff. The place has a very well-documented history. Despite its late date, the chronology might indicate something much earlier of how men were attracted to settle in large numbers—a hundred or more—in a single place. On 10th May 1881, the first brick was laid for the new settlement, made possible because Lord Hastings was prepared to sell land. He, indeed, was among the prime movers of the Central Norfolk Railway Bill. An early proposal for the railway's name was the Central Norfolk Railway; it was incorporated in the bill. One relic was the brackets of the station at Melton Constable which had spandrels with the initials C.N.R. intertwined, an echo of a railway scheme which did not become built.

The ironwork made long before the bill failed in the Commons was used. The station was in use from 19th January 1882 for trains to King's Lynn and those south to Guestwick, with through trains to Norwich from 2nd December 1882; the final section of the Eastern and Midlands Railway between North Walsham and Melton Constable was not opened until 5th April 1883. Already the village was a going concern. Twenty-eight houses for railway officers and men had been erected by 1882: the famous Melton Street. By then also there was a running shed for twelve locomotives, a coaling plant and a large turntable. The boiler shop of the works took another fourteen years to complete. By 1896, Melton Constable was complete. Colville Road was put up in 1886, and ten years later a further twenty-four dwellings were authorized, including two shops and a house for the doctor. This was larger than the others in the village. The other nineteen houses in the village were completed in 1894. In all the railway company had built seventy-one houses in a little over a decade. North of the main road the houses were developed at a more leisurely pace; these are on Gordon Road, Kitchener Road and Burgh Beck Road. The first two reveal the date, the relief of Khartoum in 1883 and its aftermath. Melton Constable had a gas-works, very much an urban innovation, from its inception. The second gasholder was added before 1889. Partly, of course, this was to cope with the increased use of fuel by the machine works, but the growth of the village meant more people were using gas. An additional water bore-hole was sunk at the same time. The grocer's shop of Mr Colman, still operated by his descendants, began in 1894. Two years later the Railway Institute was opened: some said to keep the men away from the 'demon drink'. The incomprehension about alcoholism among Temperance Reformers is baffling to the twentieth-century mind; it may have caused secondary poverty but among well-paid railway workers, especially those engaged in locomotive and rolling stock maintenance and repairs, it was a direct means of slaking their thirst. Lord Hastings seems to have realized the need to drink. The Hastings Arms Hotel, dominating one end of the village street, was there from the beginning. It had a public bar for the railwaymen.

Railwaymen lived in a benevolent atmosphere of paternalism, whoever their employer was. On the M.G.N.J., the many who lived at Melton Constable were never far from the factory hooter or the gate of the locomotive works. Even the few who worked on the land regulated their lives more by the sounds of the trains than the changes of the seasons. Another reflection of the paternalism was Lord Hastings' private waiting room on the station. He and the Yarmouth brewer, Sir Edmund Lacon, had largely financed the enterprise; the extravagance may be forgiven. It was a condition of the land sale. The nobility, of course, still dominated the countryside. There is a delightful story of a local landowner who arrived from Yarmouth one evening at Melton Constable, only to find there was no train scheduled to Fakenham at that late hour. After laying a wager with the tea-room lady of a pair of white gloves for the winner that a train would run, he was provided with a single first-class carriage drawn by a tank engine. In state Sir Thomas Cook rode home. Perhaps too his action in giving the white gloves to the loser indicates the other side of the relationship of Victorian squire to those who served his needs; he expected respect and they gave it.

The last comment is a long way from railway lore, and the M.G.N.J. has much of that, yet it does illustrate the interaction of men in Victorian England. The M.G.N.J. was an essentially Victorian creation; it belonged in a sedate world where the railway train moved at no more than three to three-and-a-half times the speed of the fastest horse, even if something nearer ten times that of the cart horse.

The railway enthusiast, of course, has a field day with the M.G.N.J. The track has gone, but stations remain and at Melton Constable there are the physical remains of the works. These one man dominated: William Marriott, engineer to the line from 1883 and its traffic manager as well from 1919 to his retirement in 1924. It was he who kept the M.G.N.J. going. The company bought some locomotives but Marriott designed and in the Melton Constable works built others. Between 1897 and 1909, neatly spanning the years of greatest prosperity for the company, these were mostly tank engines, of the 0–6–0T and 4–4–2T wheel arrangements, nine of the former and three of the latter. In 1924, the company had also fifteen 4–4–0 tender engines, dating from 1882 to 1889 and built by Beyer, Peacock and Company, as well as twenty of the same wheel arrangement built in 1894 and a further sixteen built in 1896. These pulled the express trains, both the regular ones from Yarmouth and Norwich to Leicester and that from Cromer to London, King's Cross via Peterborough, and the holiday trains from the north and the Midlands to Yarmouth and to north Norfolk resorts. Yet the locomotive stock reveals under-capitalization and consequent lack of investment in the line. No engine was less than fifteen years old in 1924, and the oldest dated to 1877. An engineer's report of 30th April 1893 noted that of the 1882 locomotives none had yet done four hundred thousand miles but one was less than two thousand off that figure. These great beasts were still going in 1924; even the youngest of them, which in five years' working had done barely two hundred thousand miles in 1893, had chalked up a mileage close upon a million. Because of the chronic under-investment, locomotives and other stock, were really turned into workhorses on the M.G.N.J. Two trips a day between Norwich and Lynn were expected of the locomotives. At 211 miles over gradients not kind to ageing steam boilers, however often they had been repaired, a lot was asked of the express locomotives. They kept going; to those who remember the railway with affection, they did more than this, they gave immaculate service.

Men speak of the maintenance carried out at Melton Constable with pride. It had to be done well; the M.G.N.J. just could not afford to replace its ancient engines. Its other rolling stock was similarly aged. Some time after the Great War, the company bought the former stock of the Great Eastern Railway built for the York to Harwich boat trains: ten coaches and two brake vans built in 1906. They ran until the early 1950s. In the nineteenth century some coaches had been built at Melton Constable. Most famous of these was the engineers' saloon, taking the inspecting officers of the company to look at bridges, the Toft Tunnel almost at the end of the system beyond Bourne in Lincolnshire, and the permanent way.

The railway had a permanent effect on the scenery of north Norfolk. The country is hilly; trains need fairly reasonable gradients so both cuttings and embankments were frequently necessary. A good series, deriving from the Melton Constable to Sheringham and Cromer line of 1887, can be seen north of the central junction of the M.G.N.J. A sinuous course, avoiding Thornage village, before reaching the southern end of Holt, the line here was single-track and without an intermediate station. Weybourne beyond officially had a station, but this was a kilometre from the village. The Midland and Great Northern Joint Railway repeated the mistakes of the firm with which it was competing. Whitwell and Reepham was not far from Whitwell Hall but distant from the more populous Reepham. Other stations on the Norwich line were better sited: Lenwade and Drayton were both in the village, Attlebridge a short walk away. On the Yarmouth line, Corpusty and Saxthorpe was actually in Corpusty: Saxthorpe is across the River Bure. The line too had conveniently sited stations at Stalham, Potter Heigham, Hemsby, Great Ormsby, Scratby, California, Caister (two) and Yarmouth New Town; the terminus was at Yarmouth Beach. For inhabitants of these villages the railway brought a great change.

Edwardian England saw a transformation in working-class habits. Holidays became possible for the respectable working class, those whose incomes permitted them to live beyond the poverty line; their jobs were steady, employment was good and their wages began to permit luxuries. One such was an annual holiday. This traffic the M.G.N.J. largely captured. It ran trains from the Midlands to the coast and transformed coastal villages north of Yarmouth into holiday villages. When in 1903, the M.G.N.J. and the Great Eastern jointly sponsored a line from Yarmouth to Lowestoft through Gorleston, Hopton and Corton, the two last-named, the northerly one of which is now in Norfolk, developed holiday camps like the northern suburbs of Yarmouth. To reach the line, trains crossed the five-unit Breyon viaduct. The M.G.N.J. had already one such viaduct, at Potter Heigham, but this was of three units, built by one of its constituents, the Great Yarmouth and Stalham Light Railway in 1879. The Potter Heigham bridge was perhaps the most distinctive echo of the attempt to bring East Anglia nearer to the Midlands.

Ultimately the "muddle and go nowhere" line failed. Railways were the innovation of the Victorian era; road transport has taken over in the twentieth century. Many lament its passing, but like all the lines of Norfolk it was designed to bring traffic to the county from afar, not serve the existing communities.

Attempts were made to bring more holidaymakers to other and different parts of Norfolk, beyond the established resorts of Yarmouth and Cromer. Both the Great Eastern and the M.G.N.J. sought to bring a train service to Mundesley, Trimingham and Overstrand; they combined to form the Norfolk and Suffolk Joint Railway. The emphasis was on the more select type of clientele. Big hotels, still in use at Mundesley, converted to other things at Trimingham and Overstrand, dating to the Edwardian era, suggest the atmosphere of Cromer. Those at Mundesley are not as overpowering in their voluptuousness as the monstrosities of Edwardian and slightly earlier vulgarity with which Cromer is saddled. The same massiveness, the same lumpiness is there. It appears too in a remarkable house in Overstrand converted by the architect Sir Edwin Lutyens for a Liberal politician made good. Cyril Flower had been Member of Parliament for South Bedfordshire from 1885 to 1893. After only eight years a grateful Gladstone gave the member for Luton a peerage. The son-in-law of a Rothschild chose as his title Baron Battersea and Overstrand. 'The Pleasaunce' looks and is hardly to our taste. Lutyens also built

Overstrand Hall, now a convalescent home, in 1899, about the date he finished his other creation.

Creation, in fact would sum up Mundesley, Trimingham and Overstrand. Despite the railway of 1898 to Mundesley from North Walsham and from 1907 along the coast from Cromer, the whole idea of this bleak coast, where the wind whistles all the way from the North Pole, as a seaside resort never caught on except with a very few. The villages remained small and undisturbed. Today there are a few caravans permanently sited, but not the innumerable hectares of rows one sees at Yarmouth or even the smaller groupings at other resorts.

Villages were not cut out to be holiday resorts, although the railway did change the character of some inland villages. The Norfolk Broads became if not big business at least a sizeable industry in the 1890s and the Edwardian era. At first converted Norfolk wherries were used; specially built ones are an innovation essentially of the years after the Great War.

The railways brought changes to Norfolk, yet in retrospect when the metals have been lifted they may not seem as great as once they were thought. For two generations produce was more easily transported to markets far distant from the county, and perhaps that was their prime function for the inhabitants of Norfolk villages. As passengers they came to use the trains less and less. Closure was inevitable. One authority has claimed that the decision about the Midland and Great Northern Joint was taken in 1948, a full decade before the system was closed or slaughtered (depending on one's point of view) on 28th February 1959. The big battalions had their way and what was quaint, and to some valuable and nostalgic, in the harsh world of economic realities prevailing in the 1940s and the 1950s lacked a subsidy. The railway map of Norfolk in 1979 looks remarkably like that of 1850, except that there is no line from King's Lynn to Norwich. There is one addition to the spine of the system: the line out to Cromer, dependent only on local traffic. There are no through trains to London and the conductor-guard asks you in an accent which is natural, "Do you want the London train?" The answer is rarely in the affirmative. Also surviving is a second line from Yarmouth to Norwich, via Acle. It follows the turnpike road of 1830, still known as "the Acle New Road", an eerie place at night, though less so now than twenty years ago. The windmills have gone, with one exception at Stracey Arms, but in the 1940s and 1950s they looked as they must have done to Don Quixote and Sancho Panza, formidable things in a darkening sky with night creeping in all around: they emphasize the bleakness of the Fleggs.

The trains, however, have had their effect here. The station at Lingwood is now set among a commuters' village of bungalows. The station at Brundall transformed a miniscule place of fifty-two inhabitants in 1841 into a village of about two thousand people today. New houses were erected near to the station in the months during which this book was being written. There are even those hardy enough to commute not to Norwich but to London from Brundall. The railways of Norfolk were built to connect the city with the capital and with the Midlands: modern-day commuters reflect the original intention for with exceptions the villages did not generate sufficient traffic for a successful local system of railways. Hence with closures, described in Chapter IX, there is now only the spine of the railways surviving.

VIII

Before the Great War

THE railway came, but by no means to all villages. Great segments of Norfolk relied still on the horse as they were to do until far into the twentieth century. At Litcham, Rowe and Son had a cycle works combined with a gramophone, electrical and ironmonger's store from the middle of the Edwardian era which still survives, as the photograph included in the plates aptly demonstrates. But in 1904 the village still had a saddler and harness maker, William Hicks Copeman, a wheelwright, William Mitchell, and two blacksmiths, George Wagg and George Henry Ramm, as well as a firm of carpenters, builders and wheelwrights, George Crispe and Sons. William Mitchell and George Henry Ramm were still in business in 1925, but W. H. Copeman had retired, his place as the village saddler was taken by H. E. Read and the second blacksmith at Litcham now had the delightful name of Christmas Burgess. The horse trades were not far different from those of 1845. Then the village had a smith and wheelwright, John King, another blacksmith, Rhoda Bridgman, and two saddlers, Abel Benjamin and James William Copeman. The son of one of them was clearly the saddler of 1904.

Yet there were differences in the villages of Norfolk between the 1840s and the 1890s and 1900s. The first was population. The population was already declining in many in the 1840s. Most villages lost men and women between 1841 and 1901. At Litcham, the numbers declined from 846 to 626; by 1921 they had declined even further to 575. At Mattishall the decline in numbers between 1841 and 1901 was more striking, from 1,155 to 746. About half-way between Litcham and Mattishall is Gressenhall

Great Ellingham

Great Snoring

Ludham

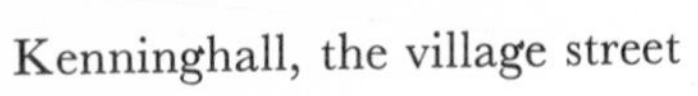

Kenninghall, the village street

Cley-next-the-Sea

Worstead

The village street at Castle Acre

Bacton

Stairway of Dairy Farmhouse, Tacolneston

Farmhouse on the green at West Acre

East Tuddenham, the parish pump

Caston windmill

where the Mitford and Launditch Union Workhouse was: it is now used as a centre for the Norfolk Archaeological Unit. The village had 957 inhabitants in 1841 but only 704 people lived there in 1901. The latter included the thirteen officers and 134 inmates of the workhouse. This itself is less than the figure for 1841 when 242 people were noted in the Union Workhouse. Numbers could vary as on 18th March 1844 there were 320 paupers in the house, while in 1800 there had been as many as 670 inmates, rather more than its capacity of 500 persons. The Loddon and Clavering Union workhouse at Hackingham, now Hales Hospital, again eighteenth century in date, was built for 510 inmates. In 1901 a mere eighty people were cared for by seven staff.

Village populations as an aggregate had declined during the Victorian years. In 1841, two thirds of the population of Norfolk lived in its villages. In 1901 the proportion was barely over a half. In both years the small towns housed about a twelfth of the county's population. The people who left the villages may have gone to Aylsham, Cromer, East Dereham, Diss, Downham Market, Fakenham, Swaffham, North Walsham, Wells-next-the-Sea or Wymondham but of these only the second, third and fourth have a significant increase in population between 1841 and 1901 while the two last-named and Downham Market have a steep drop in numbers. The villagers and those from the small towns either went to Norwich and Yarmouth or migrated out of the county sometimes abroad. Essentially during the first twenty years of the twentieth century, only Norwich and Great Yarmouth grew significantly in population, both by about nine thousand between 1901 and 1921, and the two new urban districts of Sheringham and New Hunstanton, created in 1894 and 1901 respectively, where the increases were 2,412 and 2,396, clearly the result of the holiday trade like the 1,655 increase at Cromer. Virtually the whole of the rise of Norfolk's total population between 1901 and 1921 from 476,553 to 504,293 is thereby accounted for.

New Hunstanton and Sheringham were towns created in the late Victorian years. Harmon le Strange, scion of an ancient house long-established in north-west Norfolk, saw the opportunity to develop his ancestral acres in 1862, following the arrival of the railway. Today Hunstanton looks down and watches the sun set in the sea, as do its neighbours on Norfolk's west coast: Heacham,

Snettisham, Ingoldisthorpe, Dersingham, Wolferton and the Woottons. It is an entirely Victorian creation, made popular by the recovery of the Prince of Wales, who spent his convalescence from typhoid fever in 1871 there. Ten years before he had bought Sandringham House and its estate: a major change in the villages of west Norfolk in the late nineteenth century. Sheringham is quieter, partly because men had fished from the gap in the cliffs for a thousand years and more. It is less of a single plan than Hunstanton and more human than Cromer. The big hotels, like the Grand Hotel by H. J. Green and the Sheringham Court probably by the Norwich architect Skipper, have more gaiety than Skipper's other creations, the Grand Hotel, the Hotel de Paris and the Hotel Metropole, at Cromer, all of which are later if only by a few years. The man who built the ponderous offices for the Norwich Union Assurance Company in Norwich in 1903 was obviously moving from a tiny glimpse of the spirit of the naughty nineties. He sank very soon into tasteless vulgarity. Sheringham, too, has more atmosphere than Cromer, more sense of fun and less dependence on the holiday trade. The foreigners could go away and the town would not suffer essentially because it has grown slowly to cope with the holiday trade. Even the Edwardian terraces have merit. Partly because of the close-packed nature of the town, partly due to the way the cliffs shelter it from the worst of the east wind, Sheringham has a warmth not found so easily elsewhere on the wild and windswept coast.

The building of new seaside resorts was one change in the villages of Norfolk in the late Victorian and Edwardian years. Another, equally specific, equally localized, was the purchase, already mentioned, by Edward, Prince of Wales (later King Edward VII) of the Sandringham estate in 1861. For under a quarter of a million pounds all of the parishes of Sandringham, Babingley, Wolferton and West Newton were acquired together with parts of Dersingham and Appleton. A later purchase was of a further three thousand acres (about 1,200 hectares) in two parishes to the east, Anmer and Shernborne. Upon this corner of Norfolk a benevolent paternalism was exercised. It was particularly felt in the area of church restoration. The activity was not confined to this small area, nor to the villages of Norfolk but it was marked at Sandringham and the surrounding villages. *Kelly's Directory* for 1904 is worth quoting extensively. Of Sandringham it says:

The Church of St Mary Magdalene, standing in the grounds of Sandringham House, is a small but beautiful structure in the perpendicular, consisting of chancel, nave transepts, battlemented south porch and embattled western tower, with pinnacles, containing one bell and a clock, with four dials, placed in 1899 as a memorial to the late Christopher Sykes: in the chancel are memorials to Her late Majesty Queen Victoria d. 22 January 1901 [and to six of her family]; here also are two panels of terracotta . . . and three stained glass windows erected to H.R.H. Alexander John Charles Albert, infant son of His Majesty King Edward VII and Queen Alexandra, d. 7 April 1871, and to Lieut-Col. George Henry Grey, equerry to H.M. the King when Prince of Wales d. 11 December 1874: there is also a memorial window, recently presented by the 10th Hussars, in memory of H.R.H. the Duke of Clarence K.G. d. 14 January 1892, and others to the late Rev. William Lake Onslow M.A., F.R.A.S., formerly naval instructor to Admiral H.R.H. the Duke of Saxe-Coburg, K.G., and sometime rector here, d. 30 August 1877; and to the Rev. George Brown Moxon, also a former rector; the stained glass windows in the south transept were the gift of Her late Majesty the Queen and H.R.H. the Duke of Saxe-Coburg; those in the north transept were the gift of Frederick Waymouth Gibbs esq., C.B., Q.C., M.A., former tutor to H.M. the King and the royal household, d. 1894, and there are others filled with rich Munich glass; the organ and pulpit were given by H.M. the King, and the brass eagle lectern was selected and presented by H.M. Queen Alexandra in commemoration of the recovery of H.M. the King when Prince of Wales from his serious illness in 1871–2; in the nave are suspended the old colours of the Norfolk Regiment (9th foot) and here also are memorial brasses to the late rector and to Mr Edmund Beck, late estate agent to H.M. the King; the church was restored in 1857 by Lady Harriet Cowper and again in 1890 by H.M. the King, when the transepts were added; it now affords about 100 sittings.

Adjacent churches too felt the hand of the new master of Sandringham House. Appleton was one of the seventy-two decayed churches of the county noted by the directory compilers in September 1904 and at Babingley for a population of 92, a new iron church with a thatched roof was erected at royal expense in 1894 to serve in place of the ruinous church of St Felix. For full restoration of an existing structure with the addition of many refinements, perhaps out of keeping in a country church, was contemplated at West Newton, the largest of the villages on the Sandringham estate. Sir Arthur Bloomfield did the restoration in 1881 and presented an oak lectern. It was one of the gifts noted by *Kelly's Directory*:

> The stained east window was the gift of the late Christopher Sykes esq., of Brantingham and the reredos of tiles and mosaic was given by H.R.H. the late Duke of Albany K.G.; the jewelled altar cross of brass, with two candlesticks and vases, were presented by the late German Emperor, Frederick III, and the late Empress Frederick, the alms dish by the late Lord Colville of Culross, and the rich crimson and purple altar covers by T.R.H. the late Duke and Duchess of Cambridge; the chancel is fitted with stalls of carved oak, the gift of H.R.H. the Duke of Saxe-Coburg K.G., and the pulpit was the offering of His Majesty's household; the stained west window was erected by T.R.H. the Prince and Princess Christian, the Duke and Duchess of Connaught, the Princess Louise (Duchess of Argyll) and the Duke of Argyll K.T.; there are other stained windows the gifts of H.M. Queen Alexandra, the late Grand Duke of Hesse, T. W. Evans M.D., and the royal household; H.M. the late Queen Victoria gave the fine organ, and the bible and prayer book were presented by the late Bishop of Norwich; a carved oak screen has lately been added.

Bloomfield was commissioned by Edward VII, when Prince of Wales, a couple of times more. He did his usual level of rather hideous damage at Wolferton and had a bash at Shernborne too. At the latter Edward VII gave an oak pulpit and a communion cloth; at Wolferton a stone pulpit was the chief new feature.

There is more than the churches to the villages of Sandringham, West Newton and Wolferton. Babingley is a farm and there is little enough to Anmer and Appleton. At Dersingham, royal influence was muted, but at West Newton there is a full-scale estate village. The sparkle is less than at New Houghton and less sombre than at Holkham which was rebuilt about the same time. At West Newton there are a number of buildings which are not quite effective in their message. They get better as they become more recent but the public ones suffer from a sense of being planted on the countryside, not belonging to it; one almost has a feeling of triviality about the whole place. Wolferton had its royal station, still preserved although trains no longer run to Hunstanton. Enlarged in 1898, it was a better attempt at copying the timber-framed house than many of the buildings elsewhere on the Sandringham estate.

And then there is Sandringham House, which one either likes or dislikes. There was a fire in 1891 but the subsequent rebuilding and additions made what is an important mid- to late-Victorian house look less unified than it may have been planned to be: the uppermost storey is part of Colonel R. W. Edis's additions. He also built the ballroom of 1883. There had been a plain house of about 1770 on the site before A. J. Humbert, of London, put up the main range in a Jacobean style in 1870 and before, but he retained the billiard room, or conservatory as it was built, from an earlier house. It links the house with the bowling alley, which again is older but has an upper part of 1892.

Around the house are the gardens, of varying dates. They are pleasant but a little too formal. They lack intimacy, and compared say with the garden of Holkham Hall elegance has not quite been achieved. There is a difference in approach in formal landscaping between the naturalistic style of the eighteenth century, exemplified by Lancelot Brown and by Humphrey Repton, and the Victorian creation of a park, It was the latter which drew comment in 1904: "The park is stocked with deer and the estate abounds with game, including blackcock." It is a working estate, including a stud farm for thoroughbreds noted in Edwardian directories.

Two points of interest remain from the Sandringham estate. Melton Constable had been the first Norfolk village to have its own gasworks. The great innovation of the Edwardian era was electricity. A private electrical plant was installed in 1903. It was later than the water tower of 1878, which held a tank of 32,000 gallons, fed from a chalk spring in Den Beck Wood. A supplementary storage tank for a million gallons was excavated in 1906. Norfolk villages still largely relied on wells and the village pump for their water supply.

Life for the majority of the inhabitants of Norfolk villages in the late Victorian and the Edwardian years was hard. The parish pump of East Tuddenham and the stoneware pipes of Sandringham House were worlds apart. The traditional crafts remained: wheelwright, blacksmith and saddler are found in all but the smallest villages still in 1904. The miller, too, plied his trade and by wind and by water, although steam mills had come into use. In 1904, there were no fewer than 261 millers listed in *Kelly's Directory* of whom 86 had windmills and 142 watermills, the two traditional sources of power, while there were 144 men with steam mills and two had electric mills. The figures do not quite add up because 111 millers used a combination of power, most usually water and steam, but both wind and water and wind and steam are recorded. Four mills were equipped to be driven by wind, or water, or steam. Most of the larger villages had millers, often more than one. At Kenninghall, Arthur George Fordham, a farmer, owned a windmill, while three others ran mills driven by wind and by steam. At Great Bircham, Mrs Howard, the miller, was also a baker. But to emphasize just how much Edwardian England was emphatically the last generation of rural England, a contrast can be made with the entries in *Kelly's Directory* for 1925. William Alfred Howard at Great Bircham was only a baker, while at Kenninghall there was now only one mill, worked by wind and by steam. Edgar Jolley of the same village had been one of the seven village millwrights in 1904, but twenty years later only Edwin William Daniel England of Ludham remained: three were still found in the major towns. Edgar Jolley became an agricultural engineer purely and simply, having once combined that trade with the millwright's craft.

Life too was centred on the land, but the living was nowhere near as good as it had been. The mid-Victorian years were prosperous ones for Norfolk farmers, as for others in England; but from 1873 neither wheat nor meat could make a profit. Grainlands in Canada and America drove men from the grainlands of Norfolk and the refrigerated ship from New Zealand made grazing cattle and sheep only barely profitable. What kept the inhabitants who remained in the villages was a lack of ambition, at least that is how townsmen have seen it, not understanding the pull of rural life and the attractions of a particular village to those long established there.

The majority of villagers had been content for generations to earn their livings on the land. The work was hard, menial and tedious, but it demanded an army of farm labourers. Steam-power applied to the mill, the threshing machine and the plough had reduced some of the need. New machines like early reapers and early binding machines had taken away a few more of the requirements for labour. But the agrarian revolution of the twentieth century had not yet happened: farming was not yet the lonely life of a man on a tractor ploughing a monster field in half a day or the equally lonely life of a milkman dealing with herds numbered in hundreds twice a day at an automated, electric milking parlour. Cows were driven into the farmyard to be milked by hand in Edwardian Norfolk, and the horse and the ox provided the motor power for ploughing, harrowing, reaping, binding and carting.

Their care and the rise of domestic service as employment for girls and young women kept many in the villages, but this chapter opened with the stark facts of population decline between 1841 and 1901 and this was in three of the largest villages. Farmers said that the better labour went away and blamed the village school. Norfolk villages had schools, often tiny buildings, from the 1830s and 1840s. The schoolrooms were replaced in the wake of the Forster Education Act with buildings still in use at East Barsham, at Great Snoring, at Alpington (serving Yelverton also), at Rockland St Peter (serving also Rockland All Saints) and at a host of other Norfolk villages.

The villages of Norfolk in the Victorian years were the seedbed of early trades unionism in agriculture and Joseph Arch, a farm labourer, was member of parliament for North-West Norfolk in 1885 and again from 1892. He was a Liberal and like most celebrated and self-educated men of his particular political persuasion a nonconformist too.

Nonconformity is difficult to judge in Norfolk villages. Where the chapels remain, it had strength. At Forncett End, there is a Primitive Methodist chapel seating three hundred built in 1865. The sect is the most often found in Norfolk: other villages with its chapels in 1904 were Felmingham, Feltwell, Fersfield, Field Dalling, Filby, Fincham, Flitcham, Forncett St Mary, Foulden, Foulsham, Foxley, Framlingham Earl, Freethorpe, Frettenham, Fulmodeston and Fundenhall. Felthorpe had a Baptist chapel and other Baptist chapels were found in Forncett End (part of Forncett St Peter on the road from Norwich to New Buckenham), Foulsham, Framlingham Pigot, and Fulmodeston. There were slightly more Wesleyan Methodist chapels in the county. Among the same villages Feltwell, Fincham, Foulden, Great Fransham may be noted while Field Dalling had a Free Methodist chapel and Filby a Unitarian one. With their emphasis on preaching, loose parochial organization, heavy reliance on the laity and few ministers, the Victorian Methodist and Baptist congregations gave opportunities for men to shine. Qualities of leadership were brought out, powers of public speaking developed and the ability to organize learnt by participation.

As a forum for religious observance they differed considerably from the parish church. Something of the flavour of the late Victorian and Edwardian church may have been gleaned from the comments on Sandringham and West Newton. Victorian Norfolk and its villages had an orgy of building in churches and chapels. The latter were financed by the sweat of men's brows; the restoration of the parish church was paid for as a memorial to a loved one, as a thank-offering for deliverance, almost as an expiation of wealth. Victorian church restorations vary. Some are incredibly bad; others are plain, serviceable and in a way to be admired. Hemsby church is like that with its nave roof copying the old medieval roof. Winterton church too has a Victorian roof, a single span over 10·37 metres (34 feet) constructed in 1878, which neither excites nor depresses. Yet there are Victorian church restorations which do excite. Martham church is unashamedly Victorian and proud of it. The whole of the chancel was rebuilt in 1855 by Mrs Dawson, widow of a vicar of Rollesby and daughter of George Pearse, vicar of Martham from December 1834 to 1861. She used Philip Boyce of Cheltenham as architect and a very good job he made of it too. The east window cannot be other than a restoration yet it seems not without character; about the Easter Sepulchre memorial to Jonathan Dawson it is possible to be neutral yet the stone pulpit ranks with the best in the land. The whole thing is lavish: it cost £8,000, including the rebuilding of the hammer-beam roof in the nave. The latter ends at the chancel arch, within which a series of secondary curves has been placed. Philip Boyce, who also did work in Leeds and in Barnsley, deserves to be better known.

At Necton, far away from Martham, there is another good Victorian restoration, with a lantern spike copying that at Shipdham erected above the tower of 1865. And at Framlingham Pigot the more commodious structure given in 1859 to replace a three-cell Saxon church is no mean piece. Henry Christie employed a decent architect, Kerr, and his efforts if destructive in one sense leave a lasting impression. He knew what he was about and that was providing a suitable house of God.

Perhaps the lasting impression of Norfolk villages in the last quarter of the nineteenth century and the first decade of the twentieth is left by another parish church: Booton. The Rev. Whitwell Elwin, the parson, was his own man and for good measure designed and built at his own expense the village school and the vicarage as well. He stuck it out as parish priest for fifty years and after twenty-five of them took up architecture and in a curious way succeeded. Certainly the comment made by Sir Edwin Lutyens, "very naughty, but built in the right spirit", can be disregarded as jealous. It is not strictly correct as to the principles of Early English style but at least the man had a go. He was not going to be outdone by his neighbours, the churches of Cawston and Salle, and he made his point. No one in the twentieth century would dare.

IX

The Twentieth Century: Past, Present and Future

THE Great War is distant past, yet it remains a convenient break for a general book between the historical and the contemporary. In villages people still stand in silence for two minutes on the Sunday nearest to the eleventh day of the eleventh month; they still hold that respect for the eleventh hour of that day. The memorials went up, one for every village, noting the men who died. On England the effect of mass death was shattering; on small communities it was cold-blooded and brutal. A quarter of a generation was wiped out. At Yelverton they noted the ages of those who did not come back from the trenches: 20, 20, 33, 34, 24, 22, 23, 34, 21, 37, 18, 27, 25, 19, 32; six of them fought with the Norfolk Regiment, two with the Essex Regiment, and one each with the Inniskilling Dragoons, the Lancashire Fusiliers, the Middlesex Regiment, the Oxfordshire and Buckinghamshire Light Infantry, and the Royal Engineers; two served at sea. The sentiment of the time was expressed by the commemorative words of the plaque inside St Mary's Church, Yelverton:

> In memory of those who so willingly and freely gave their lives for their King and Country, fighting for the cause of freedom, justice and honour to secure for the world an everlasting peace.

Thereafter Norfolk villages were never quite the same.

The years after the Great War and before the next seemed changeless but the changes which accelerated after 1945 have their roots in the 1930s. It is a long time since 1918. No man who fought in the Great War is less than eighty; few who served in the Second World War are aged much under sixty. Villages in Norfolk have a group of surviving monuments in common: church and war memorial are two. The village sign-post is a more recent addition.

Between 1918 and 1978—the time is sixty years: two generations, almost three—two massive contrasts stand out: religion and railways.

In 1918, almost every village had its own vicar or rector. I say almost every village because the holding of livings in plurality and the uniting of benefices is not unique to the twentieth century. Framlingham Earl and Framlingham Pigot were held together for much of the nineteenth century. Today, Framlingham Earl is combined with Poringland: three churches but that at West Poringland is little used. Framlingham Pigot, the Victorian replacement for a perfect three-cell Saxon church, is part of the Bramerton group of parishes. There are eleven churches in the group sited west of Loddon on the road from Beccles to Norwich. North of the road is Bramerton itself, Ashby St Mary, Rockland St Mary, Claxton and Carleton St Peter; Thurton is astride the main road, while to the south are Bergh Apton, Yelverton and Framlingham Pigot. Four clergy serve the group, assisted by four lay readers. Each church manages a service each Sunday. East of Loddon is another group of parishes: the Raveningham group. Here not every church has a Sunday service every Sunday. The rota is elaborate, giving Stockton only two Sundays with a service: Evensong on the third Sunday of each month and a communion service on the morning of the fourth Sunday of each month. Within this area, at least one church is closed: St Margaret's, Hales. It is a two-kilometre walk from the middle of what is a growing village. No one, it seems, wishes to take on the tenancy of Church Farm adjacent.

South Norfolk is not alone in this amalgamation of parishes into groups. The area between North Walsham and the sea provides a good example: the Trunch group. Three clergy with the assistance of three lay workers and a retired clergyman serve the needs of ten villages: Antingham, Bardfield, Gimingham, Knapton, Paston, Southrepps, Swaffield, Thorpe Market, Trimingham and Trunch itself. Here the policy on services is a single service in each church during the morning: 09.00, 10.00 and 11.15 are the commonest times. Four times a year the whole group meets at 10.30 for joint worship.

Two problems have contributed to the contraction of church services: the declining population of Norfolk villages and the overall problem of the decrease in Anglican clergy. Given the available personnel, and the shift of people to the towns, only the largest villages can now have their own vicar. And there are very few Norfolk villages which have a clergyman both resident and serving a single community: Bradwell is one, but this overgrown suburb of Great Yarmouth (to take the most uncharitable view) houses over two thousand people. Church services seem lavish in their provision, almost, one is inclined to add, archaic: early-morning holy communion, mid-morning family service or parish communion, and a traditional Evensong.

Away from the Fleggs, only Sculthorpe seems to be as amply served but here the Victorian parish church does duty also for the adjacent Dunton as well; the latter has no church. Villages like Martham, Winterton and Hemsby all manage the full series of services, with also at Hemsby a Roman Catholic Mass celebrated each Sunday during the summer. At Winterton, the rector conducts a daily celebration of holy communion, itself a rare act in the late twentieth century.

Of other persuasions, Methodism has stood the test of the twentieth century's indifference to religion rather more solidly than the older nonconformist creeds. Over much of rural Norfolk, nonconformity never took hold. There is a Congregational chapel in Briston, an exquisite late-Georgian example with the minister's house attached. Another Congregational chapel is that at Yaxham, but at Shipdham the village uses the former Congregational chapel of 1881 as a United church being both Methodist and United Reformed Church in its ministers. Elsewhere it is the Methodist chapel which stands and is much used. In the Trunch group of parishes at Southrepps and in Trunch, itself, and on the coast road beyond there are thriving Methodist chapels at Lessingham, Scratby and Hemsby. Martham has its Methodist chapel and a Baptist one also. More rarely found are Baptist chapels. Caister-next-Yarmouth and Bacton are villages on the coast road with services maintained at the Baptist chapel. Others are Brooke and Foulsham, both again larger than average villages. More often only in the small town, as at Loddon, are both Methodist and Baptist chapels found. A whole string of villages from various parts of Norfolk could be quoted with the Methodist chapel surviving as a living entity. At Bradwell two Sunday services are held; sometimes it is only one service. East Harling, Besthorpe, Bawdeswell, Drayton, Sculthorpe, Bodham and East Runton were all villages noted on a day's journey with a Methodist chapel. At East Harling, the Quaker Meeting holds a monthly devotion in their building.

With their form of organization very different from that of the Church of England, the nonconformists are able to keep going precisely because they do not have the encumbered weight of tradition which besets the Anglican Church. Clergy are not individually beneficed. Some have secular jobs. Much of the preaching and the taking of services is in lay hands. Rare indeed is the disused chapel in a Norfolk village. There are some, of course. One I have seen is that built in 1850 for the Wesleyan Methodists at Tivetshall St Margaret; another is the tiny forlorn building, of unknown denomination, out far to the east of Kenninghall which is now a farm barn. In terms of loss of buildings, the nonconformists have been more fortunate than the Church of England. Tivetshall St Mary and Wiggenhall St Peter are two which the twentieth-century church has abandoned. It has rebuilt too: a restoration in 1928 at St Andrew's Church, Claxton, and more specific renewals after disasters at Bawdeswell and Little Walsingham. At Bawdeswell, All Saints' Church is in a neo-Georgian style, very light and airy, which neatly complements the brick frontages of the village. At Little Walsingham the parish church of St Mary was burnt down on 14th–15th July 1961, leaving only steeple, south porch and the Sidney tombs. It might have been more kind to have rendered safe the great gaunt ruin and left men to stand and stare for the restoration does not inspire the author.

Railways in 1918 reflected the achievement of the previous two generations. In 1978 they have been reduced from the intricate web of sixty years before to merely the main lines from Yarmouth to Norwich and on by the Ipswich route and the Cambridge route to London. Branch lines for villages have been reduced to the line to Cromer and the two ways to Yarmouth, all originating at Norwich. But few are the villages directly served by these lines. Stations serve Brundall, Lingwood, Acle, Cantley and Reedham on the Yarmouth lines, and on the Cromer line much less effectively Salhouse, Wroxham, Worstead, Gunton and West Runton as well as North Walsham, Cromer and Sheringham among Norfolk's towns. Effectively the village station is a thing of the past. All were there in 1918. Only one, Ashwellthorpe on the short connecting spur between Forncett and Wymondham, had gone before 1948, a casualty of the reduction of passenger services with the onset of the Second World War: through trains from London to Wells ceased to be run.

The early 1950s saw the first batch of closures: Tivetshall to Beccles ceased to have passenger trains on 5th January 1953 although goods services lingered on for another decade. The total closure of the Wells to Heacham line came on 30th January 1953. There had been flood damage to railways before, but hitherto the lines had been repaired. The most serious began on 26th August 1912 when 175 millimetres of rain fell in twenty-four hours. For the Midland and Great Northern Joint Railway very detailed information has been published. The line took a month to re-open and two weeks further for a full service to be restored. At Thuning Bridge the rails were left in mid-air as they were at Banningham Bridge and at Hellesdon. The cost of repairs was £20,000. Yet with the next flood, that of 1953, the railways except on the coast were more fortunate. When the sea burst its banks with terrible and devastating effect on coastal towns and villages, the railways were shattered only once. The stations at Sedgeford, Docking, Stanhoe, Burnham Market and Holkham had already closed their doors to passengers on 12th June 1952. All traffic ceased on the line; the flood removed any hope of keeping the metals laid.

It may be because they were such an early closure that the stations remain in these villages. One, Stanhoe, has the usual disadvantage of being two kilometres from the village, but like Docking and Sedgeford it was intact in 1975. The remoteness of the area leaves much to survive, like the level-crossing gates at Sedgeford and the goods shed at Docking. The early closure also illustrates the great loss of jobs a railway closure brings: five stations only, but each with a small staff and two signalmen for the signal box. Only thirty kilometres but almost certainly it employed as many men. Even on railway lines still open the loss of manpower is as great. The branch to Cromer is the best illustration of this. Crossings of railway over road are now worked automatically; the weather-boarded crossing-keeper's house accompanying each remains, sometimes tenanted by the former railway employee but more often sold to another. One of the few crossings still operated manually has a modern house in place of the old. At stations there may be a single employee still on duty, as at Worstead, but often there are no staff. The majority of the buildings at Gunton station have become a private house with the platform for a patio. Railway travellers use the opposite side, without buildings.

The largest railway closure in Norfolk was that of 2nd March 1959 when the Midland and Great Northern Joint Railway became not just a name of pre-war days but a thing of the past. Melton Constable to Sheringham lingered on to 1964 and there are still pay-trains from Sheringham to Cromer. Bits also retained freight services for up to another decade but the line derisively called "Marriott's tramway" was shattered: truthfully, it had outlived its usefulness.

Forty Norfolk stations were closed; thirty Norfolk villages lost their trains. They had been under-used for years. This was the largest axe. By the time of the famous Beeching Report in 1963 there was essentially little left to chop off from the limbs. Cromer to Mundesley had closed in 1953, thus depriving Overstrand and Trimingham of stations; Mundesley, itself, saw the last passenger train at the end of the 1964 holiday season and the last freight wagon the following Christmas. At the same time goods trains were withdrawn from the Hunstanton line; Wolferton, Dersingham, Snettisham and Heacham continued until the early summer of 1969 as passenger stations. Other closures following Dr Beeching's comments were those of the lines from Fakenham to Wells, depriving the Walsinghams of their station, and from Thetford to Watton and Swaffham. For four years thereafter it was still possible to travel from Norwich to King's Lynn by train direct, although usually a change in East Dereham was necessary. But on 3rd September 1968 the last trains ran on the metals west of Dereham and the last passenger trains too on the line from Wymondham to Dereham and Fakenham. Great Ryburgh, North Elmham, Yaxham, Thuxton and Hardingham all lost their trains, as did East Winch, Narborough, Dunham, Fransham and Wendling.

At first the state-subsidized omnibus company, Eastern Counties, ran its services to meet the villagers' needs, but the use of the bus declined as that of the train had declined. Like the train, the bus can only survive if it attracts sufficient customers. And that is unlikely. The author has sat in solitary state on more than one country bus in Norfolk: on the early-morning one from Great Yarmouth to Loddon, on one at lunchtime from Trunch to Mundesley, on an early-afternoon one from Corpusty to Cawston although as a longer journey from Holt to Norwich that did have half a dozen passengers from the first to Melton Constable and again picked up people going into Norwich for the afternoon.

The reason, of course, is the motor car. More Norfolk people *per capita* are car owners than anywhere else in England. With sparse population—the county in 1971 had 617,616 inhabitants, but of these 121,688 live in Norwich, 50,236 in Great Yarmouth and 30,107 in King's Lynn—the omnibus company fights twenty years later the same battle that the railway fought and lost.

At Hardingham, in northern Breckland, the area formerly covered by the Mitford and Launditch Rural District Council, the Eastern Counties Omnibus Company ceased services as it had in other villages between East Dereham and Wymondham only eighteen months after the railway closed. In August 1977, *The Times* highlighted the problems of the declining village using Hardingham as its example. Transport inadequacies were a major complaint voiced by the residents. There were only two bus services a week, and according to the most recent timetable one of those no longer appears to operate. The villagers are left with a single service, operated privately, each Friday into East Dereham. Hardingham is not quite the extreme case it may seem. There are no buses whatsoever at Reepham, a failed market town. At Thurlton, the quality of the service is the subject of frequent complaints in letters to the *Yarmouth Mercury*. In this remote village, where the road is barely of sufficient width for a bus, there is one service a week to Beccles, one to Norwich, and two to Great Yarmouth. The latter, on Wednesdays and Saturdays, do not take the main road but go via Belton. For living in such a village a car is an essential.

For living virtually anywhere in Norfolk, a car is an essential. The bus services have been reduced to a series of radiating spokes with Norwich as the hub of the wheel. One every two hours on most routes would appear to be the norm, and in some cases not even this. Except on Saturdays there is no mid-morning service from Norwich to Fakenham. Attlebridge, Lenwade, Bawdeswell, Bintree and Foulsham rely on a service designed to get people into Norwich in the morning and out again in the early afternoon and in the evening. In 1978 the bus arrives in Norwich at 07.25, 08.30; 15.10, 15.50, 17.52 and 19.58 with an additional mid-morning arrival except Thursdays, a slightly later one which does not run on Mondays and Wednesdays and a further early-afternoon arrival which does not operate on Fridays. Eight times are given for the journey from Norwich, again with lunchtime complexities as to the days of operation. In some ways the service from Norwich to Fakenham is better than most; there is a late-night bus, for example, which is not always found. Villages on the route from Norwich to Holt and Blakeney have a late-night service only on Wednesday to Cawston, on Friday via Cawston and Edgefield to Holt, and on Saturday to the same through Cawston and Melton Constable. Cawston is a thriving village: the population increased from 944 in 1961 to 1,171 in 1971. Yet the bus service into Norwich, 16 kilometres (10 miles) away, is seven per day. Melton Constable is beyond Cawston; in contrast it is a declining village. In 1961 there were 670 people living there, but twenty-five fewer in 1971, and former shops stand empty, a gaunt monument to a vanished prosperity the railway brought. The bus service is poor, even by rural standards: three per day from Holt into Norwich with four return journeys, and a term-time bus into Fakenham. The latter service has an additional, early afternoon, journey to Fakenham on Tuesdays, Thursdays and Fridays. The basic reason is the lack of custom; a greater provision would increase the level of subsidy required from the rates.

The difficulties of not being a car-owner in a Norfolk village are considerable. Only in those villages such as Mattishall and Yaxham, to the west of Norwich, Multbarton and Newton Flotman on different roads to the south, and Poringland and Thurton on different roads to the south-east of the city, is the service good. Here the bus is part of a longer service, one which connects Norwich respectively with East Dereham, with New Buckenham, with Ipswich, with Bungay and Southwold and with Beccles and Lowestoft. In West Norfolk there is much less emphasis on the village bus. A few routes radiate from King's Lynn, but only on the service to Wisbech and Peterborough through the Tilneys and the Walpoles, and to Hunstanton via Castle Rising, Dersingham,

Snettisham and Heacham, is the service operated at more than hourly intervals. The long journey from King's Lynn through Great Bircham, Docking, Stanhoe and Burnham Market to Wells-next-the-Sea is only covered by two buses each way each day but here the population is sparse. The former Docking Rural District Council area, covering the north-west corner of the county, lost nearly two thousand people between 1961 and 1971. Only the coastal villages of Dersingham and Heacham have increasing numbers; only Snettisham in addition had a stable size. Eight parishes in 1971 had under a hundred people living there, double the number of a decade before.

The great blank area around Fakenham and to the west is provided with a bus service only on Thursdays and Saturdays: the former is market day in the local town. And then the provision is one bus into Fakenham in the morning and one out around lunch-time. Even so there are villages without any bus at all. Great Snoring is one and since it is high, even a fit man balks at carrying a load of shopping the three kilometres (two miles) from East Barsham or the five kilometres (three miles) from the single stop at Little Snoring. To live in Great Snoring one requires a car for survival.

Survival is measured in other ways: with the very young and with the dead. To take the dead first. Perhaps the best sign of a healthy village is the need for a new graveyard. There are village churchyards, overgrown, unkempt, untended, and not yet full. Forncett St Mary has one like this. There are other villages where a new plot for the dead has had to be found. Hemsby and East Rudham are two such villages, while at Wood Dalling, Shropham, Sculthorpe and Forncett St Peter the village churchyard has been enlarged. At the last, however, the approach to what is the finest of the Saxon round church towers in the county is through a forest of grass. Tombstones, paid for by long-dead widows and off-spring, lie choked in weeds. The problem is not peculiar to any one village. At Yelverton a flock of sheep were being used to eat their way through the spring growth in 1978. At East Tuddenham, the sunken approach to the porch was being cut with a scythe but a later visit showed that only this was done, together with the portion of the churchyard, itself beyond the old bounds, now in use as the village burial ground. Edwardian and Victorian dead, they lie in peace with their ancestors, although here no eighteenth-century gravestones were to be seen. In most villages, all of whatever persuasion lie together by the parish church. At Kenninghall, however, the Particular Baptist Chapel, erected in 1807, had its own burial ground; no tombstones later than the Victorian years could be observed in the plot around the chapel.

Both early and late in Victoria's reign, landowners and interested parsons were assiduous in providing village schools in Norfolk. At Scoulton a public elementary school was erected in 1840 for 40 children but as the average attendance by 1904 had reached 50 another classroom for a further 35 children was added. At Hardingham, the school celebrated its centenary in 1962; 10 years later it closed. There were only 18 children between 5 and 11 years old. In 1904 the average attendance had been 95 in a set of classrooms built for 130. It cost £1,300 to build with the master's residence and was enlarged in 1883. In 1892 a clock with a bell was erected by the parishioners in memory of the lady who paid for the school, Miss Edwards. At Cranworth, 83 children in 1904 attended a school built for 120 pupils 60 years before. At the beginning of the twentieth century there was even a school in tiny Wood Rising with a population of 102. For comparison the people of Scoulton numbered 293, those of Hardingham 426 and at Cranworth 228. Today only Scoulton has a school. At Cranworth and Wood Rising closure came as it did to the schools at Whinburgh, at Garvestone which served Thuxton also with its 53 children in 1904, and at Kimberley where there were only nine pupils in the same year. Deopham and Hingham had schools too and these like that at Scoulton have remained open. For the children of Hardingham and for those of Cranworth, Wood Rising, Whitburgh, Garvestone, Thuxton and Kimberley, the school bus became a feature of life. They board at 07.30 and return home at 16.00. It is a long day. The faces of the children are drawn with tiredness before the school day begins at 09.00 in Hingham or in Shipdham. For a five-year-old the strain can be too much.

The situation is not confined to north Breckland. In the northern part of Lothingland, there are two first schools in Bradwell and a middle school and a school in Belton but Burgh Castle, Fritton and St Olaves have no schools. The convoy of school buses may be seen each day in term-time. During the vacations the children are in their own village and a semblance of normality returns. But visit a village without a school anywhere in Norfolk and a sense of emptiness is present. It is wrong to expect people to live in a world without children. The contrast from villages where the school survives and thrives is immense. At Great Snoring the sound of the playground is heartening. There may not be many pupils in the school built in 1859 for a hundred pupils but their voices make up for their lack of numbers. The happiness they have does not make the old saying of schooldays being the happiest of a person's life any less true; it enhances the truism. In the old Walsingham Rural District Council area there are thirty-nine civil parishes, including Fakenham. Of the rural ones, eighteen have schools for children under 11, twenty do not. Some are fairly obvious combinations: at Great Walsingham the children go to school in Little Walsingham and those of Little Ryburgh attend the school in Great Ryburgh while Hempton is on the fringe of Fakenham. Yet remote villages like East Barsham, Little Snoring, Hindringham, Hindoloveston, Brinton, Field Dalling and Langham retain their schools.

For Wood Norton, Warham, Stiffkey, Morston, Binham, Holkham, Helhoughton, Swanton Novers, Thursford, Gunthorpe, Kettlestone, and Wiveton the village school has closed its doors. Only Helhoughton, a single solitary place from those listed, had more people in 1971 than in 1961. People do not want to live where their children depart each day early and return late. The whole area is declining in population, yet the planners, the office workers in Norwich, the thinkers who seek to direct lives by moving people to where it is administratively convenient should not think in terms only of neat tidy boxes of people set down in concentrations of useful sizes. It is often those who deny individuality to others who squeal the loudest when even the tiniest piece of their own individuality is threatened. The decisions which closed schools were not always taken in the 1970s; some date to the 1960s, some even to the 1950s. Yet the depressing thought remains that people who live in suburban estates with neighbourhood schools and a convenient row of shops, a nearby public house, a garage selling cut-price petrol, assume that everyone is the same and wants the same impersonal lives that so many lead.

Impersonal is what the Norfolk village never is; yet the town-dwellers, the theorists, the examiners of maps (they go under many less complimentary names) seek to obliterate individuality and replace it by the crude impersonality of the town. The enemies of village life exist in many guises. Almost invariably they work for large urban-centred organizations with minds schooled in the profit-and-loss account and the tidiness of bureaucracy. They produce huge and expensive structure plans, lavish in their printing, seemingly impressive in their presentation yet totally motivated by facile solutions. They look so tidy on paper; the classifications are so neat and they are easy to administer. The thinking reduced to its bare essentials demands an acceleration of the process whereby inconvenient little communities of under two hundred people are killed off, painlessly. First remove the village school. It is an easy solution; no young couples will buy a house in such a village. Yet surely the whole process has gone too far; it needs to be reversed. There is no justification whatsoever in educational terms for closing a school with eighteen pupils. There may be only one teacher, all ages might be taught together but these are a small price to pay for individual attention and improved standards.

It is incontrovertible that children suffer because of daily herding on to the school bus; they cannot relate to their own environment; they have become creatures of an alien world with homes and school divorced from each other when they should be in unison. The complete balderdash and codswallop—to adopt the vernacular that is native to a Norfolk man—spouted by educational theorists has had too long a day and ruined too many good village schools and the villages of Norfolk have suffered.

The damage caused by the loss of the village school might be irreparable, although the caring person hopes not. The other losses, not directly caused by the thinkers of an oversized bureaucracy, merely indirectly, may individually not be damaging but cumulatively they almost certainly are. Public house, shop, post-office, even regular church services (by which is meant at least one service every Sunday), these have begun to disappear from the villages of Norfolk and the world has become the poorer. *Kelly's Directory* in 1904 had very few places, except the most miniscule, without at least one public house per village. There was often a choice of houses, some with a name and some merely a beerhouse. Like local authorities, breweries have their own urban bases and it is not easy for the village pub to survive. When it does it is often one of two extremes: the dingy beerhouse out in the wilds, where a man hesitates to take his girlfriend, or the swish country pub where the prices are often fancy and where the trade is geared to attracting the outsiders, at least to the lounge, where the food is good but not cheap, and the investment is distinctly for the non-village trade. There seems to be no happy medium between the two. The village pub, however, does not always remain. The inhabitants of Hardingham do not have one, although before 1900 there were three, and two in 1904; the last closed in 1968 with the railway: it was attached to the station. At West Acre there was no public house in 1904, nor is there one today. If that at Hardingham, The Railway Arms, has become a transport café, the former King's Head at East Harling has become the village post office. Beer will no longer flow from their pumps.

The village shop too has gone, often in the same places as where the public houses have all closed. At West Acre, the sixteenth-century timber-framed farmhouse, now boarded up, which fronts the village green has a large and prominent notice suggesting it should become a village shop. The idea is sound, for a community of 221 people should be able to buy their groceries locally and not have to drive into Castle Acre, four kilometres (two-and-a-half miles) to the east. The alternatives are East Walton or Gayton, if not King's Lynn or Swaffham. Only perhaps with approaching a thousand people will there be more than one shop as there is in Castle Acre or in Bradwell.

The village post office is often combined with the village shop. At West Acre it is not, but a house has adapted its front room to serve. Its existence does mean that pensions can be collected by the old, stamps bought by the young and the not so young, allowances collected by mothers of young children. Above all the village post office, like the village pub and the village shop, serves as a social centre where news can be exchanged, the pleasantries of life developed, and gossip circulated. The closure deprives the village of its centre for informal contact. And closure is a decision taken by tidy minds far away who see a lack of profit and decree that the limb should be hacked off. It is difficult for a villager to be other than incomprehending about the savagery with which the Norfolk village has been treated by the last generation of officials. The unvoiced thought is: what are the rates paid for; the unspoken question is: why do the bureaucrats exist. The answer to both is distinctly not the destruction, aided and abetted by governmental authority, of the Norfolk village.

The preceding paragraphs describe how many inhabitants of Norfolk villages see the destruction of their environment, in places as diverse as New Buckenham, Blakeney, West Bilney, Little Barningham, Bergh Apton and Burgh St Peter. The view is too often expressed to be real. And the most recent local government reorganization has not helped. It has made the towns dominant. It has made the process of government remote. The individual plan for an extension to a cottage in Kenninghall can only be inspected in East Dereham because that is where the planning office is. It is a long way from Kenninghall to East Dereham and there is no bus except by going into Norwich.

Norwich is a single authority; Great Yarmouth another. The villages on the Fleggs and in northern Lothingland were amalgamated into the town. These two make both geographical and administrative sense. West Norfolk is centred on King's Lynn, but it has hived off a miniature county from the rest of Norfolk. On the 1971 population figures the district has a population of 110,002. It is surprising that it was not made larger by including Swaffham and the area of the Swaffham Rural District; only another 14,865 would have been added to the population. As it is, the area of the Swaffham Rural District has been incorporated in the Breckland District. Here Thetford, Swaffham, East Dereham and Attleborough compete to be top dog among the towns. Yet Wayland Rural District, with Attleborough and Thetford, are more part of south Norfolk and little different in thought and outlook to the area called South Norfolk. Of the parliamentary constituency which these form, 80,195 people live in the modern district, 13,727 in Thetford (formerly a municipal borough) and 20,554 in the old Wayland Rural District. As it is, Breckland District has the smallest population of any of the five districts to which the majority of Norfolk villages belong. Of its 76,404 inhabitants, almost half live in one of Thetford, Swaffham or East Dereham. The urban balance is tipped when Attleborough is included as a town. In modern North Norfolk, towns do not dominate but the population is small, only 74,227 on the 1971 count. Yet the logic of the concept of a single authority from Horsey to Holkham is not immediately apparent, even in terms of coastal defence and against pollutants. What, if anything, do the inhabitants of Hickling have in common with those of Helhoughton? The whole of local government's post-1974 set-up looks to be the product of a mind which had a fixation with the minimum size of seventy thousand people and sought willy-nilly to impose this on the immensity of Norfolk. It would have made much more sense to have put together the areas of the Walsingham Rural District and the Mitford and Launditch Rural District and the two former urban districts of East Dereham and Wells-next-the-Sea. But the chances of redrawing the local government map are highly remote.

Even if they were to be redrawn, the probability is that local government would seem remote. The close relationship of people and their rural district, as developed certainly in areas as diverse as those of the Mitford and Launditch Rural District and the Depwade Rural District, was shattered by the intervention of the 1974 reorganization and its emphasis on towns and their hinterlands, and by its concerns first and foremost with townspeople not villages and their inhabitants. The earlier arrangements had been very different.

From 1894 all the villages of Norfolk were administered in a three-tier system: the Norfolk County Council, established in 1888, at the top, a middle tier of rural district councils and the parish, either with its own council or for the smaller places a parish meeting. The system worked as well as any system can. No place under 4,000 inhabitants could be created a town, in the administrative sense. Thus among the more prominent of the old market towns, Aylsham, Fakenham, Holt, Loddon, Harleston, Attleborough, Hingham and Watton did not become urban districts. They remained part of the rural district which had its offices in the town, rarely in the village. But the rural district was only the old Poor Law Union under another name. And that was often two Domesday hundreds combined as with the Loddon and Clavering Union which was the two hundreds of those names with, additionally, the parish of Yelverton to form forty-one parishes. They had secured an act for their combination in 1763 and built a house of industry at Heckingham in the same year. It served as the workhouse and is now Heckingham Hospital. Also in South Norfolk, twenty-three of the parishes of the ancient Forehoe Hundred secured an act in 1776 for the maintenance of their poor. They built a house of industry as Wicklewood; it cost

£11,000 and is still used as a hospital. One parish in Forehoe Hundred, Honingham, was not in the original union. In 1834 it was added to the existing St Faith's Union and subsequently has been part of the Aylsham and Saint Faiths Rural District and is now among the parishes of Broadland District. Logically this parish which straddles the River Tud belongs with the rest of its fellows from the old hundred. In the early twentieth century Forehoe Rural District functioned on its own, but it was too small and from 1935 it was combined with the adjacent Henstead Rural District. Henstead Union, the predecessor, was two ancient hundreds: those of Humbleyard and Henstead. In the Waveney valley on the north bank, a poor law union was formed in 1835 amalgamating two of the ancient hundreds, Depwade and Earsham, with most of Diss Hundred: Bressingham, Fersfield, Roydon, Shelfanger and Winfarthing were included in the adjacent Guiltcross Union, dissolved in 1902. Later these were part of the Depwade Rural District. Its offices were where the workhouse was: Pulham St Mary Magdalen, also known as Pulham Market.

From Forehoe and Henstead Rural District, Loddon Rural District, Depwade Rural District, Diss Urban District and Wymondham Urban District, the South Norfolk District was formed on 1st April 1974. The administrative headquarters were sited in Farthing Green House, Loddon; public health and housing were henceforth to be dealt with at Hill House, Pulham Market; and the engineer and surveyor had his offices at Long Stratton. The planning and treasurer's departments are at Norwich. One rural district before 1974 had extensive offices in Norwich: Aylsham and Saint Faiths. For South Norfolk collection offices are provided at Wymondham and Diss and at Harleston. Meetings of committees take place in Loddon. Farthing Green House, a veritable mansion in the attractive small town, has that air of dignity which local government ought to provide. But for meetings of the full council the representatives meet at County Hall, Norwich. New offices, in a futuristic style, are being provided at Long Stratton which is as central to the area as one can get.

But as with the closure of the Midland and Great Northern Joint Railway, local government reorganization had one unforeseen consequence: it enhanced both the pull and the dominance of Norwich. Norfolk villages live under the shadow of their county capital. It is there as the centre of bus routes. For all except West

Norfolk, it is the major shopping centre, although inhabitants of the Fleggs do tend to shop in Great Yarmouth. The twentieth century and its affluence has bred the need for major shopping centres. Norwich added this to the many roles it already has.

A book entitled *Norfolk Villages* might theoretically be expected to say little of Norwich; that is right, yet at the same time it is wrong. Two points stand out: one, purely of the twentieth century, concerns the spreading tentacles of the city; the other is older. No city which had good claim at one stage in time to be the second city of England can be other than what Norwich is. The city is a collection of villages. Thirty-two parish churches of the Church of England survive although many are not so used; four more were victims of the Second World War. One other was demolished in 1887, and in the early eighteenth century another twenty could barely be remembered: Francis Bloomfield quoted them as no longer in evidence. Few, except St Peter Mancroft, are large and the dedications reveal an amazing variety of saints. Yet to St Michael three remain, to St Peter four but, of the last, one is that demolished in 1887. St Peter Hungate (now the museum) and St Peter Parmentergate, St John the Baptist Timberhill and St John Maddermarket, the names ring out as though of tiny communities who stood there to worship God as the Middle Ages closed. Their compactness recalls the village churches of Norfolk. Around them a little community once lived, and indeed continued to live, for the city did not burst its encircling walls until after 1789 and mass housing did not move out for another century.

Today the city spreads far beyond walls and the River Wensum, far indeed beyond the encircling ring road built in the 1930s to keep the traffic out of the city. Lakenham, Eaton and Earlham, all once villages on the River Yare, are already within the city bounds. Theoretically, because they are beyond the ring road, Thorpe St Andrew, Sprowston, Catton, Hellesdon and Costessey are outside the city boundary, yet they are not really different from suburbs of Norwich. With Costessey the feeling grows every time one passes the construction site at Bowthorpe. Clover Hill, the placards proclaim, is a "pleasant place to live", yet with its construction the land west of the city between the Rivers Yare and Wensum becomes another urban zone.

The Royal Norfolk Showground at Easton is probably the

barrier: it is a fair drive from Mattishall or East Tuddenham, from Honingham or Hockering. Yet each of these suffers from being a commuters' village, to a greater or lesser degree. On the road to Fakenham, north-west from the city, the tentacle is longer. Hellesdon, virtually a mere suburb of Norwich, gives way to Drayton which in turn is followed by Taverham. In each there is a sense of the inhabitants wanting both the best of village life and the advantages of the town. North and north-east of the city, Norwich Airport, Beeston Park and the woods beyond Sprowston effectively mean Norwich keeps within its new bounds. The same is true in the vale of the Yare and round to the south, although Cringleford is fast losing its own identity. Here the attraction of Norwich is different, the distance people choose to place between home and work greater. On the road to Bungay, Framlingham Earl and East Poringland provide suitable homes for those who wish to drive to work. Beyond is Brooke. Rockland St Mary, on another road, east of Kirby Bedon and Bramerton, is no different in scope, but Brooke is the better example of a commuters' village at a not inconsiderable distance from the place of work.

Far away in West Norfolk, Great Massingham stands very much in the same relationship to King's Lynn as does Brooke to Norwich. Down Lynn Lane, there is a long straight road across Grimston Heath and north of Grimston village to Roydon, and on across the wildness of Roydon Common to the roundabout where the coast road crosses the more direct route from King's Lynn to Cromer. Here the commuter has two routes, through South Wootton north into King's Lynn, the way the bus goes, or south along the far end of the coast road to the bypass south of the town.

From Brooke there is a long straight road into Norwich, and there is only the untidy sprawl of East Poringland and Framlingham Earl to slow down the fast car. Norwich is a fifteen-kilometre (ten mile) journey; Great Massingham to King's Lynn is half as much again. South of Brooke is the emptiness of the farming area of South Norfolk. Seething, Mundham, Thwaite St Mary, Kirstead, Hedenham and Woodtun earn their livings from the soil; the same is largely true of Shotesham and Saxlingham Nethergate to the west and, for that matter, Stoke Holy Cross and Caistor St Edmund between them and Norwich.

These commuters' villages stand out. Housing is one of the

great denominators of such a village. It may be good or, and often to commentators more usually is, bad. One group in Brooke is particularly striking, a number of large red brick detached houses, the sort of thing which developers and estate agents term 'executive houses' (with all the hideous connotations that implies). These seven are better than average, grouped round a brick dove-cote standing beside a brick wall separating the close from the churchyard. The houses have all the accoutrements of the financially successful: double garages for the occupants' cars, room for the twentieth-century's technology of living like the deep-freeze refrigerator, the colour television, and the multi-farious laundering gadgets. They have all the marks of affluence, and the same may be said of similar, but perhaps slightly less well thought out, houses in Rockland St Mary and Great Massingham. At the former the most expensive houses have room for the parking of the owner's caravan or his boat, although perhaps the latter would be stationed at Rockland Staithe.

These houses and some less well designed ones found south-west of the Norwich to Bungay road in the other half of Brooke are the type which encourage expatriates from the towns to make their homes in villages. The west part of Brooke is less attractive than the north-east part. Here there are fewer of the old houses, and only the rather unattractive Baptist chapel of 1831, now covered in a nasty grey cement. There are more of the modern houses here too, and these follow the penchant for the neo-Georgian and reflect the dominance of ideas which cram people into small spaces. Still this should not detract from the north-east part of the village, a street splitting either side of the twin village ponds, the northern one of which was being cleaned in August 1978. Here older houses face the centre, including some as old as the latest parts of St Peter's Church. Porch House is quoted as mid-seventeenth century, but might be some generations older. It is the largest of the old houses, and is at the end of the trees and the ponds, on the southern side. The north side is not broken by a road like that opposite. Here the more attractive old houses stand. Left alone Brooke would survive as an epitome of an "old world village" even if, like the rectory, most of it has no greater antiquity than the eighteenth century. Some houses possess the quiet dignity of that age.

One must ask what the commuting element does for Brooke.

Some residents obviously just tend their gardens and go to work, but it is a thriving village with its own society, The Brooke Society, to keep it together. It has changed much over the last century and more. One does not now recognize the village decribed by William White in 1845:

> A large and well-built village, Brooke has 756 souls and 2,049 acres of land, belonging to many proprietors, some of whom have neat mansions here, the largest of which have well-wooded parks, viz: Brooke House and Brooke Hall. . . . In the village is a Baptist Chapel, built in 1831. A large National School has been built here for the parishes of Brooke, Howe and Kirstead.

Howe and Kirstead still send their children to school in Brooke. In 1971 they had respectively 56 and 206 inhabitants; Brooke had 1,025, somewhat more than the 695 recorded ten years before. That is the influence of the commuting element in the population.

Men and women do not earn their livings in ways that in 1845 seemed both ageless and changeless. There were 13 farmers in Brooke then, including 2 with the surname Bridges, 2 named Chase and 2 called Tibbenham, while the 4 grocers included a John Tidnam, and a George Tidnam was one of the 4 shoemakers. The village had tradesmen of other kinds: 2 saddlers, 3 tailors, 2 plumbers and glaziers, a wheelwright, a blacksmith, a joiner and a sheep dealer. James Whirr was a bricklayer, and ale could be supped at two beerhouses and the more elevated King's Head, the inn on the main road which also served as the post office. The latter has not moved far: it is now in a shop beside the inn and adjacent to the village cross-roads. The world of early Victorian villages was neatly captured at Brooke. A more elevated strand in society was there: a corn miller, a veterinary surgeon, two surgeons. Gentry were there, too: the vicar, another clergyman of the Church of England and the Baptist minister. The last-named is to be excepted, but the two others could, if a little deferentially, take sherry with the lord of the manor at Brooke Hall, another clergyman, or with George Samuel Kett Esq. of Brooke House.

The same society was visible in 1904, a full decade before the Great War. The Holmes family still had Brooke Hall and John Holmes, J.P., was lord of the manor. Brooke House had changed hands: Viscount Canterbury owned its lands but the house was the residence of William Robert Mills. There were other gentry:

John Brigham and his daughter at High Green House, Mrs Anderson at Welbeck House remote from the main part of the village, J. E. Cooke at Brooke Lodge, and G. E. Gillett at The Hollies, together with the vicar. But the profusion of clergymen had gone, a noticeable change between the Victorian and the Edwardian village. The gentry had their recognizable servants, gardeners and estate carpenters, now noted in *Kelly*'s *Directory*. This in its 1925 edition could also note the chauffeur, the gamekeeper and the gardener to the new owner of Brooke Hall. Tradesmen too in 1904 and 1925 reflected the changed world from 1845. The largest group were farmers, but there is a significant difference between before and after the Great War. In 1925 *Kelly*'s *Directory* noted "the land is now the property of the various tenants"; the estates of Holmes and Viscount Canterbury had been broken up. By 1925, the big houses had new residents: Brooke Hall was owned and lived in by Major A. L. Bruce, M.C., and Brooke House had become the residence of another military gentleman although owned by another. Other houses too were coming to be owned by new residents: Wallace King at Porch House, H. S. Basden at The Hollies, John Motts at High Green House, Mrs Parfitt at Mere House, Henry Williams at the Shrublands and William Tidnam at Bay Cottage. His father had been a farmer at the same place. New trades came in: a cycle repairer, market gardeners, fruit growers, smallholders, and the range of work done by the plumbers, painters and glaziers expanded. Traditional men remained in 1925: the wheelwright, the blacksmith, the carpenter and the harness maker.

Half a century later these are not to be found in Brooke, nor in many of the villages of Norfolk. The Norwich area telephone directory (which excludes West Norfolk) does not have wheelwrights among its classifications; there are barely a dozen blacksmiths in the villages and village saddlers have been reduced to two at East Ruston, near Walcott, and at Fersfield. Even carpenters have been reduced to sixty-four entries in forty-two villages.

The change in land-ownership after the Great War, followed by the decline of the traditional crafts and their replacement by agricultural engineers of whom eighty are listed by the telephone directory, has brought about change in the villages more momentous than any change in the previous millennium. The present-day directory does not list inhabitants of the villages by their occupation. Most do not earn their livings there. They ply trades like accountancy, banking, customer relations, draughtsmanship, engineering, and so on through pop group's road manager, public relations consultant and panel-game quizmaster to xeroxgraphic reproduction equipment salesman, yacht designer and the other zeniths of the twentieth century's multifarious professions.

Their lives and their concerns are far removed from the inhabitants of Norfolk villages even as recently as 1890. The rector of one village, Scarning, could find nothing admirable to say of the Norfolk man. He wrote:

> The East Anglian is, of all the inhabitants of these islands, most wanting in native courtesy, in delicacy of feeling, and in anything remotely resembling romantic sentiment. . . . Always shrewd, the Norfolk peasant is never tender; a wrong, real or imagined, rankles with him through a lifetime. . . . Refinement of feeling he is quite incapable of.

Some Norfolk residents think that of foreigners and interlopers; some, long established in their village, think that of newcomers. Except for the shrewdness of mind, all Norfolk residents would reject the Rev. Dr Jessopp's high-handed judgements; the man from Lady Margaret Beaufort's foundation did not take the trouble to know his parishioners. Perhaps a chaplain in ordinary to Edward VII could not be expected to be sympathetic to his flock. The Norfolk village has changed a lot since then.

The rector is no longer resident, and sometimes he does not reside in one of the parishes of his charge. The farm labourers' cottages have become the desirable, almost bijou, residences of outsiders. This many resent, and they have a point. Equally the charge that small boxes are built to form retirement homes for those from far away, but often of Norfolk origins, is not unjustified. There is a sense in which the peopling of Norfolk villages with only the retired makes for an unbalanced population, especially if the village is one where the school has been closed. But the twentieth century has not yet become the century of the directed man—and long may it not be so; it remains the century of individualism, the century when the ordinary man has achieved economic independence. With this economic independence has come the freedom to choose where he will live and no one should criticize those who, having spent a lifetime of toil in unlovely Luton, brutal

Birmingham, or overpowering Oxford, should wish to return to the county of their birth or seek to set down new roots in that most tranquil of counties, Norfolk. Their experience can enrich the life of the Norfolk village. More often than not the newcomer or the returning retired meets with nothing but courtesy, kindness and friendliness and the children of such become accepted equally as village residents, even if their stay is limited to a few days at a time. One does not find the inhabitants of a Norfolk village "wanting in courtesy".

The change from the land and its livelihoods as the basis of the village to retirement and tranquillity as the desired attributes has brought problems. If there is no shop, no post office and no public house, there may be only the weekly meeting of the over-60s club to use the village hall, except for the harvest supper or in 1977 the Silver Jubilee tea. Anyone who observed the villages of Norfolk in 1977 could not help but be struck by their continuing vitality: the new village sign of Helhoughton is one permanent reminder. Village signs belong to the twentieth century; many date from the Coronation year, 1953, and others are the result of work by the local Women's Institute or, in the case of East Harling, winning the best-kept village competition. Villages are well kept in Norfolk.

Undoubtedly the biggest change in Norfolk villages in the twentieth century has been in housing; the same is true over all of England, urban as well as rural. The change has not merely been improvement: cottages were still being built without indoor sanitation, running water, and certainly without bathrooms when Edward VII spent his summers at Sandringham. They were built like that in the villages of the Sandringham estate: people had not yet learnt the need to raise basic standards. Change came, later in Norfolk villages than elsewhere, in ownership. Before the Great War, home ownership for the majority was unknown. In the late twentieth century it is the norm. In Norfolk there are still tied cottages which go with the job on a farm. The railway ones, better than the majority of their fellows in the villages, have been sold off. But the people who rent a house rather than buy one have become council tenants.

In some ways it is an impersonal system: the tenant deals with an office in a town, anything up to ten kilometres away. As with Gillingham, there may be another town, in this case Beccles, only

Victorian chancel of Martham church

Boats in the staithe at Rockland St Mary

Farm labourer's cottage, built 1845, at Hemsby

Victorian houses in the hamlet of Brundish, near Raveningham

Melton Street, Melton Constable

Briston Road, Melton Constable

Salle school

Edwardian shop at Litcham

Haddiscoe High-level station built 1936, abandoned 1968

Wroxham station, 1978

Council housing of the 1930s at Tacolneston

Council houses designed by Tayler and Green, 1954, at Hales.

Seventeenth-century dovecote and close of detached houses of the 1970s at Brooke

Bungalows at Bradwell

a kilometre or a little more over the river but in another district or another county: Beccles is in Suffolk, but like Bungay and Lowestoft is much used by Norfolk people. These include inhabitants of the much-praised council houses of the former Loddon Rural District Council. Wherever the traveller walks in the area he comes across clusters of houses looking, in a sense, above average in quality. They are found over all the parishes of the eastern part of South Norfolk: at Woodtun, at Ditchingham, at Hedenham, at Thurton, at Ashby St Mary. Tayler and Green, the architects, began their work in 1947 and tried, they claim, to get away from the conventional. Mockmile Terrace, Haddiscoe, is an early terrace with different coloured walls for each house. Set back from the road it is unremarkable, except in its date, 1949. Kells Acres, Geldeston, is of the same date and incomplete. This does not look too bad but another unfinished scheme, that at Brooke, is distinctly tatty. The injection of the colouring material into the oldest schemes as at The Warren, Claxton, was nothing short of disastrous. The whole image is tarnished and most unpleasing. Equally hideous in its effect is St Mary's Row, Aldeby, right opposite the bus stop. It faces a small green and would look much nicer in good, honest red brick. Another terrace in the same village, of identical houses, looks so much better for being left alone.

The sense is left that the architects found a formula and did no more than adapt it each time they were called upon to provide a new group of houses. They did it successfully in one village. Using crescents and closes, an isolated group of twenty dwellings was grafted on to three pairs of pre-war council houses at Church Road, Bergh Apton. A small green and trees are retained, as they are often used effectively elsewhere. The Bergh Apton group is 1950 and 1956 in date and has both single-storeyed co-joined dwellings and more conventionally designed two-storeyed terraces. The colour is a wash rather than a different brick; the facings are blue, yellow and light red. Each house has a different hue, often anaemic to the author's taste. But obviously someone liked them, for this was a scheme which gained an architectural award.

The ideas are different, the individual houses fairly well planned: they have that in their favour; but the schemes exhibit both sameness when viewed in the mass and a lack of inspiration after the first flush of enthusiasm. And for the first one seen, those in Hales, a second look produced a very different reaction to the muted approval initially engendered. Ignoring the architectural critics' preference for terraces and being objective about the whole corpus of work by Tayler and Green, the houses at Hales strike this observer as the most out of place group he has seen. Hales lacks a village centre; there is no focal point. The now closed church of St Margaret is far out in the fields to the south, on one side of the Loddon to Beccles road. On the other side of the road is Hales Hall and Hales Green; east of the village is the workhouse, now Heckingham Hospital. The latter does not quite dominate but the development of 1949–54, known as The Boltons and Gardenside, does not, as Sir Nikolaus Pevsner thinks, form a new village centre.

By far the most successful scheme of houses by Tayler and Green is the largest and the only one in which the whole setting is urban, for Loddon is a small town rather than a village. Here the housing provided includes an estate of twenty-two single-storey dwellings: the Gravel Pits group is an old people's community. An eighteenth-century wall is retained and exposed. The architects could rise to building on a much larger scale: seventy-eight houses in George Lane, Loddon, and its neighbours. The estate has no right angles, the groups of houses are linked by walls, but the walls are patterned brickwork and use trellis and bargeboards on the houses. As with the first of these estates they make it seem habitable and not just a dormitory. Perhaps the whole would not work in a larger town, but this estate suggests that the more vacant expanses of mass post-war council housing could have been avoided.

Yet the whole ethics of architectural experiment are raised by the work of Tayler and Green. Is the countryside the right place to conduct such excursions into architectural adventure? Norfolk villages may not always be the place for such experiments. Certainly the same architects' use of small-scale flats at Burgh St Peter in white brick and in a box-like style with cubes for bay windows on the upper floors hardly succeeds in producing a favourable response. More cheering is Hannover Square, Mulbarton, set out on Long Lane, nearer Bracon Ash than Mulbarton. It does look like a community, grouped round a courtyard with all the doors inside the development, and with a row of single-storey dwellings to the west. As a piece of architectural composition, the group of "executive houses" set against the brick wall of the churchyard at Brooke and retaining the dovecote as the centrepiece is far more excellent than the council house schemes.

But behind the latter was private finance, not corporate provision which decrees the conventional wisdom should not be individual in its approach. Low-cost housing, say the well-informed critics, must never have space in which to breathe, must never reflect the four acres and your own cow philosophy. It was the latter which governed the thinking of rural district councils before the Second World War. The majority of council houses in Norfolk villages were built between 1928 and 1936, although the Loddon Rural District Council built some in reddish-pink brick at Hellingdon Corner in 1938. At Shipdham, the Mitford and Launditch Rural District Council built three pairs of red brick houses with gable-ends in 1929, two pairs in 1930, two pairs in 1931, and also in 1933 and in 1934, while in 1934 they built two pairs of similar plan but with half-hipped roofs in 1936. The development south of the village also includes a pair erected in 1936 and some later pairs, including the same style built after the Second World War. Very similar houses were built as semi-detached farm cottages at East Bradenham in 1945. The Mitford and Launditch Rural District Council's style is found in two pairs of 1930 and two of the following year at Yaxham, while those on the western edge of East Tuddenham are of 1926. The same council built at Mattishall in 1930 and 1931, at Lenwade in 1931 and 1935 and at both Hockering and North Tuddenham in 1928 to 1930. These are the most honest and the best examples of the thesis of large allotment spaces round the houses. The choice of material, red brick, was good; it has weathered well and conveys the settled feel of central Norfolk in a most evocative way.

The gardens here could hold another house, as they could equally in what is undoubtedly the most pleasing group of council houses in a Norfolk village, those with pebble-dash walls coloured yellow at Tacolneston. They seem to complement the much older farmhouses of the village. But these are semi-detached pairs of houses, often looking like the older-style hall-and-crossing house, and it is to pairs that fashionable architectural critics object. Yet, as I have already observed, terraces do seem out of place in villages.

Of course, not all council housing of between the wars has either the stark honesty of the work of the Mitford and Launditch

Rural District Council nor the prettiness of those at Tacolneston. There are council houses with grey exteriors. Sometimes it is unbelievable in its starkness, as with those erected in 1936 by the Walsingham Rural District Council at Sculthorpe which seem unnecessarily barren. Yet the same treatment of grey pebble-dash in the houses of the Fleggs Rural District Council at Winterton-on-Sea of 1925 and a little later emphasizes the harshness of the wild and windswept coast. The same is found at Caister-on-Sea, again not without justification although here the suburban feeling is not entirely absent. Roses around the door and well-trimmed gardens go a long way to improving even the most bleak house, if not to suggest a pretty country cottage. There are some particularly well-kept ones at Winterton-on-Sea.

Council housing for those who live and work in the villages raises another problem. The older property has been bought up by outsiders and the only houses young families can find is the state provision. Opinions differ on whether that is right. To the families long established in Norfolk villages, even if shifting in their exact home, there is a strong sense of injustice that the roots can only be continued by living in someone else's house, but against that must be set the fact that for centuries the farm labourer rented, not bought, his cottage. However, all have the right to share in the twentieth century's unprecedented prosperity, not only those who do fashionable jobs in Norwich, or work in the energy industries of oil and gas.

If one never knew Bacton before the gas terminal came a comparison cannot be made; if the space had not been filled in 1957 would it have remained wild like Winterton or Waxham or would it have succumbed to the holiday invasion? Coastal villages in Norfolk are subject to pressures that were largely absent in the Edwardian era. Industrial man has leisure and holidays, and their scale is unprecedented. The Broads for many have already been ruined; the coast remains largely untouched. The scars are there, noticeably in Hemsby, Scratby and Caister but the villages prosper on the excellence of their sands. Semi-detached houses offer spare rooms for bed and breakfast letting, imitating Great Yarmouth and its boarding-houses. A caravan park and leisure complex occupies much of Caister and there are smaller versions of the same at Hemsby and Scratby.

The sea, however, is not always kind. At Winterton, the most central part of the beach is dangerous for bathing. And all of the coast could have been swamped in oil from a disaster. By sheer coincidence this book was written between the collision which produced the *Eleni V* disaster and the report on the procrastination, the delay, the stupidity, the waste in time, manpower and effort which so nearly sent five thousand gallons of crude oil on to the beaches and the golden sands. The pollution came; it was black sludge, horrific in its death toll of marine life and seabirds, frightening in the potential for economic disaster it so nearly brought. By sheer coincidence again another disaster on another coast happened as this book was being completed; the speed with which authority sought to deal with the *Cristos Bitas* which threatened St Bride's Bay, Pembrokeshire, contrasted with the lack of alacrity in dealing with the *Eleni V*. A Norfolk man cannot but notice these things. Does a coast beautiful in its bleakness and providing the livelihood of thousands matter less than another?

Authority in London seemed to be of that frame of mind. Similarly it is defence not beauty which rules another portion of the village coast. No bathing is possible at Trimingham and Sidestrand: the mines laid in the Second World War have not been lifted. Beyond is the bleakness of Cromer and the different and more beautiful bleakness of the marshes which go all the way past Blakeney Point and Scolt Head to Brancaster Bay and Gore Point. Yet above this as above all of Norfolk another danger lurks. Never singly, always in pairs, as if afraid to hunt death alone, they come. One moment the sky is clear, only the sound of the birds can be heard; the next second the piercing scream, the shattering crescendo, the deafening roar as the sound barrier breaks. Like monster birds, the killers hunt, their nuclear missiles visible as they swerve and straighten, performing their manœuvres; a sane man asks if this is not too high a price to pay for peace. No day in Norfolk seems to be without the hideous reminder. The twentieth century has not been a peaceful century.

The chapter began with the Great War. Whole villages were devastated for airfields in the Second World War. There were two near Norwich, at Weston Longueville and at Haveringland, both now closed, while a third, at Coltishall, remains open. Closed too are the airfields at Little Snoring and at Great Massingham: the honours board from the former is placed on the west wall of the village church, an intimate reminder of death and glory. Still used are the airfields at Sculthorpe and at West Raynham: from here the harbingers of destruction still fly their deadly missions, a single missile now more lethal than whole squadrons of wartime bombers. A whole area of Norfolk lies devastated to what the Ordnance Survey poignantly called in large red letters "Danger Area". No one now lives at Tottington. Where the trees have not taken over the Breckland, the tanks roam freely and the firing ranges are there to be avoided. Here because of its strange, unreal use, the bleakness that was once most of Breckland remains. Thompson Water would be more beautiful if it was away from bullets; as an oasis of calm adjacent to Madhouse Plantation this lonely place reflects exactly the insanity of permitting the wild places of the world to be devastated.

Norfolk villages have much of the county's wild places. The whole of the county north of the Yarmouth to Norwich to King's Lynn road (the modern A47) could be designated "the great emptiness". The coast is wild and windswept. Wild, too, is Breckland, the true Breckland about which Olive Cook wrote so evocatively. With so much wildness, with so much emptiness, with so much beauty there are few large villages. The sense of time is more precise and present as it should be, looking both forward and back. Backwards it shows how short is the span of a person's life; how much a single generation must be the guardian of the heritage it has received, how much the same generation has to give to carry forward the whole of the village to its successors and for its children's children and beyond. It also says how short-sighted are policies of devastation either for private profit or for public gain, if either is what it is.

These policies demand an end to beauty; they are the products of uncaring minds. Urban, exploitative, they demand too much of the world's resources and they give back too little. The calmer life of the Norfolk village gives back to the earth more than it puts in. Any man who has farmed a single hectare, or watched a field being ploughed, seeded, drilled and harvested, knows instinctively how much can be taken out and how much must be put back. The agribusiness of the twentieth century may treat the earth with machinery even the Edwardians would have found frightening in its complexity. It certainly employs a single man where once half a dozen were needed. But the twentieth century's agrarian revolution has been more fundamental than its eighteenth-century predecessor: it has made two ears of corn grow where only one before was raised. Farming lies still at the heart of Norfolk villages. The change is that it is now capital and technology which dominate, not labour. The change should be recognized that the modern farmworker has at his fingertips skills no factory hand has ever understood. He needs not just the age-old attributes of an eye for the weather and a nose for the ground; he must know about fertilizers and finance, about diseases and diets, about machinery and milking-parlours.

The suspicion remains. We live in a beautiful land. Norfolk villages convey, if not a sense of the picturesque, a beauty born of a thousand years of life, a millennium of man's eternal struggle. It is a far more deeply felt beauty than the superficial. It changes much across the fourth largest county of England. Below South Lopham where the River Waveney almost meets the River Little Ouse and a single thin sliver of road joins Norfolk to the rest of England there is the same feeling of independence as there is on Mundesley beach. To watch the sun set in the sea at Dersingham or Snettisham and rise again at Sea Palling or Caister is to experience a feeling that this independence matters.

To do well is "to do different"; it is an old Norfolk saying which sums up the villages of Norfolk. They want to survive. They will survive, not just as pleasure centres for the newly affluent, not just as retirement havens for the work-weary, not merely as dormitories for the more highly placed of twentieth century society. They will survive, thrive not perhaps as before, but then it was a thousand years from the burial of Sir Thomas Browne's "sad sepulchral pitchers" to their discovery and the Norfolk village was a very different place in each of these. It is a very different place today from what it had been in the seventeenth century, or for that matter in the nineteenth. A generation hence another could write another book and record another thirty years of life; it will be as different as is the life today from that sixty years before. The view remains that it will still be a village life far beyond the twenty-first century.

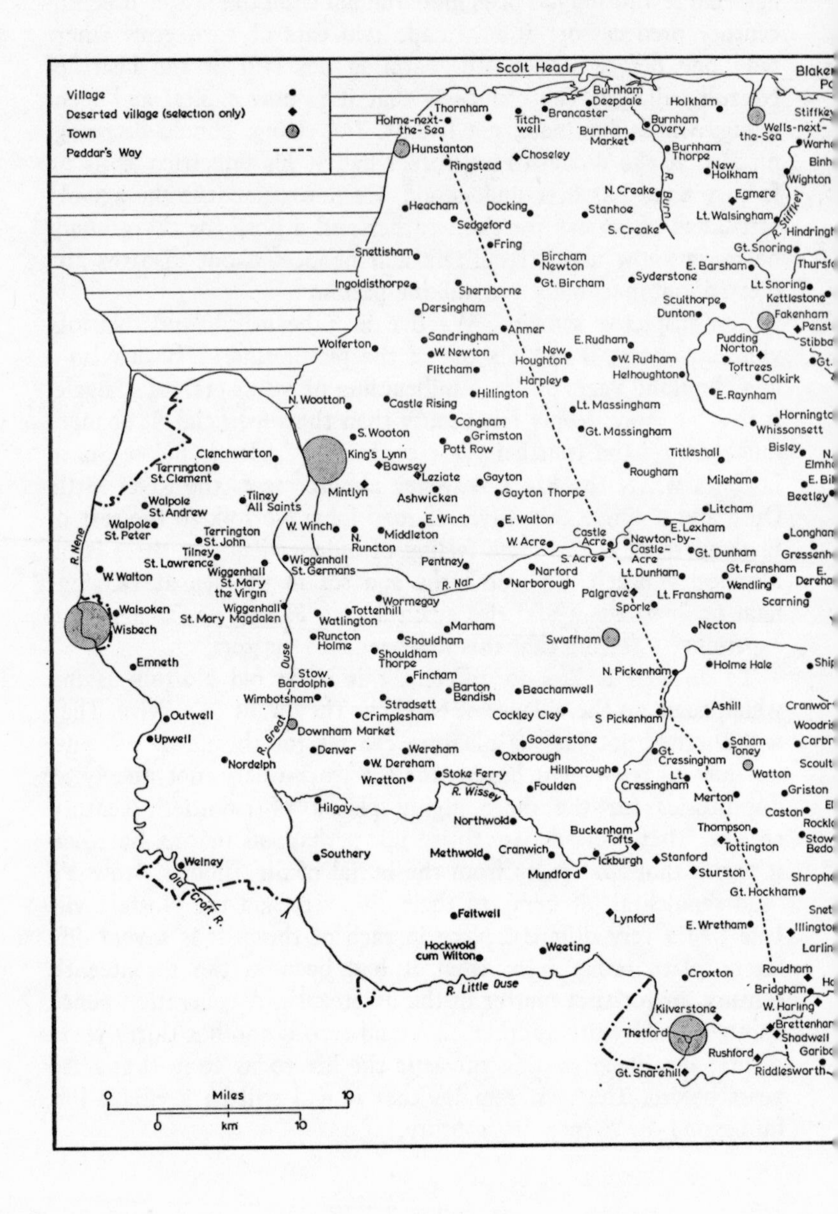

Village
Deserted village (selection only)
Town
Peddar's Way
Scolt Head
Thornham
Holme-next-the-Sea
Titchwell
Brancaster
Burnham Deepdale
Burnham Market
Burnham Overy
Holkham
Wells-next-the-Sea
Hunstanton
Ringstead
Choseley
Burnham Thorpe
New Holkham
Wighton
N. Creake
R. Burn
Egmere
Heacham
Docking
Stanhoe
Lt. Walsingham
R. Stiffkey
Sedgeford
S. Creake
Fring
Snettisham
Bircham Newton
Gt. Snoring
E. Barsham
Gt. Bircham
Syderstone
Lt. Snoring
Ingoldisthorpe
Shernborne
Kettlestone
Sculthorpe
Dersingham
Dunton
Fakenham
Anmer
Sandringham
E. Rudham
Pudding Norton
W. Newton
New Houghton
W. Rudham
Wolferton
Toftrees
Flitcham
Helhoughton
Colkirk
Harpley
Hillington
E. Raynham
N. Wootton
Castle Rising
Lt. Massingham
Congham
Horningtoft
Whissonsett
S. Wooton
Grimston
Gt. Massingham
Pott Row
Bisley
Clenchwarton
Tittleshall
King's Lynn
Terrington St. Clement
Bawsey
Rougham
Gayton
Leziate
Mileham
Mintlyn
Walpole St. Andrew
Tilney All Saints
Ashwicken
Gayton Thorpe
Beetley
Litcham
Walpole St. Peter
E. Winch
E. Walton
W. Winch
Terrington St. John
E. Lexham
Middleton
Castle Acre
N. Runcton
Newton-by-Castle-Acre
Tilney St. Lawrence
W. Acre
Gt. Dunham
Pentney
S. Acre
Wiggenhall St. Germans
Gt. Fransham
R. Nene
Wiggenhall St. Mary the Virgin
Narford
Lt. Dunham
W. Walton
R. Nar
Wendling
Narborough
Wormegay
Palgrave
Scarning
Lt. Fransham
Walsoken
Wiggenhall St. Mary Magdalen
Tottenhill
Sporle
Watlington
Marham
Wisbech
Necton
Runcton Holme
Shouldham
Swaffham
Emneth
Shouldham Thorpe
Holme Hale
N. Pickenham
Stow Bardolph
Fincham
Barton Bendish
Beachamwell
Wimbotsham
Ashill
Stradsett
R. Great Ouse
Cockley Cley
Crimplesham
S Pickenham
Outwell
Downham Market
Upwell
Gooderstone
Saham Toney
Denver
Wereham
Oxborough
Gt. Cressingham
Nordelph
W. Dereham
Hillborough
Watton
Wretton
Stoke Ferry
Lt. Cressingham
Foulden
Griston
R. Wissey
Hilgay
Merton
Caston
Northwold
Thompson
Buckenham Tofts
Tottington
Cranwich
Southery
Methwold
Stanford
Ickburgh
Welney
Mundford
Sturston
Old Croft R.
Gt. Hockham
Feltwell
Lynford
E. Wretham
Hockwold cum Wilton
Weeting
Croxton
Roudham
R. Little Ouse
Bridgham
W. Harling
Kilverstone
Thetford
Shadwell
Rushford
Gt. Snarehill
Riddlesworth
Miles
0
10
km
0
10

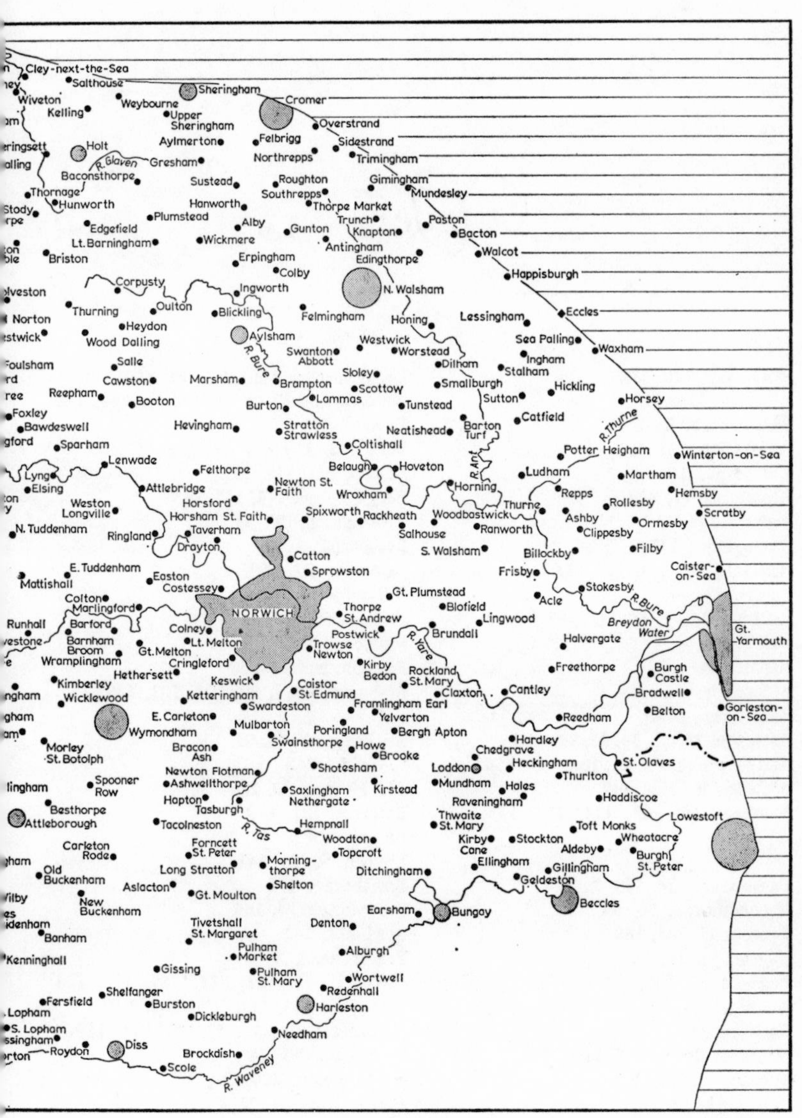

Based with permission on Ordnance Survey, Crown copyright

Index